CHINA-EU TRADE DISPUTES AND THEIR MANAGEMENT

CHINA-EU TRADE DISPUTES AND THEIR MANAGEMENT

Kong Qingjiang

China University of Political Science and Law

NEW JERSEY · LONDON · SINGAPORE · BEIJING · SHANGHAI · HONG KONG · TAIPEI · CHENNAI

Published by

World Scientific Publishing Co. Pte. Ltd.

5 Toh Tuck Link, Singapore 596224

USA office: 27 Warren Street, Suite 401-402, Hackensack, NJ 07601

UK office: 57 Shelton Street, Covent Garden, London WC2H 9HE

British Library Cataloguing-in-Publication Data
A catalogue record for this book is available from the British Library.

ISBN-13 978-981-4273-40-4
ISBN-10 981-4273-40-6

In-house Editor: Agnes NG

Typeset by Stallion Press
Email: enquiries@stallionpress.com

Printed in Singapore by World Scientific Printers.

PREFACE

Since China's accession to the WTO, China and the EU have witnessed dynamic growth in trade relations. The EU has become China's biggest trading partner and China, the EU's second biggest trading partner. Concurrently, bilateral trade relations with the two has emerged as a significant feature of the international trading system, with China being the world's most populous and second largest economy and the EU being the world's largest market. In the wake of the ongoing global financial crisis and against the backdrop of surging trade disputes between China and the EU, it is thus timely and useful to assess bilateral trade relations between these two powers, which are two very different types of international actors, with different economic and regulatory structures, and even value systems. This book is an attempt to identify the factors that are contributing to the trade disputes which have become part of, and have an immense impact on China–EU trade relations, and to address the issue of managing the surmounting trade disputes.

CONTENTS

ACKNOWLEDGMENTS

The Author would like to thank *Global Trade and Customs Journal, European Business Law Review* and their publisher, Wolters Kluwer Law & Business, for their authorization to reprint his articles (Chapters 9 and 4 respectively) in this book.

He would also like to thank Agnes Ng and the staff of World Scientific Publishing Co. for their professional services and patience.

The author acknowledges that the book is supported by a Wuhan University International Law Institue project (08JJD820169). It is also part of a project supported by Zhejiang Gongshang University Procedure Law Centre.

CHAPTER 1

TRADE BETWEEN CHINA AND THE EU: A HISTORICAL PERSPECTIVE

This chapter attempts to review the history and the present status of the relationship between China and the European Union (EU)[1] and to examine the existing problems and issues, with a view to illuminating the context of the trade disputes between China and the EU.

I. A Retrospective Account of the China-Europe Relationship

Trade between China and Europe began many centuries ago. Traditionally, while China exported silk, porcelain and other luxuries to Europe, little of what Europe could offer was acceptable in China, partly due to the tyranny of distance, as well as the self-sustaining economy of ancient China. The Opium War of 1840, which itself was a result of the greed for trade opportunities on the part of a European nation, i.e., England, ushered in a century of conflict between the two civilizations and a sense of humiliation on the part of the Chinese.

When the People's Republic of China was founded in 1949, the two powers did not grow closer. Their relationship was affected by their

---

[1] The EU, an economic and political organization, is the progeny of the European Community (EC). On 18 April 1951, France, Germany, Italy, Netherlands, Belgium and Luxembourg signed the treaty of the European Community of Steel and Coal (ECSC), which entered into force on 25 July 1952. On 25 March 1957, the above-mentioned six countries established the European Economic Community and the European Atomic Energy Community. In 1965, the three communities merged into one European Community. The Maastricht Treaty entered into force on 1 November 1993, and the term 'the EU' was replaced progressively with the term 'the EC'. In this book, the use of the terms of 'the EU' and 'the EC' are not strictly distinguished, and the term 'the EU' is used most often.

1

respective relationships with the US and the Soviet Union. A cold relationship was observed between China and Western Europe before the Sino-American rapprochment took place. This alignment of China and the US in the early 1970s against the Soviet Union brought about a change in China's relations with Western Europe. It was not just Western European countries which individually established formal diplomatic relationships with China in the years after 1972, but also the European Economic Community as a whole.

The rest of this section reviews China-EC/EU relations in three distinguishable periods.

The First Period: From 1975 to 1989

In 1975, China and the European Economic Community reached an agreement on the establishment of formal relations. Initially, both sides did this in order to enhance their own international standing.[2] From the Chinese point of view, the partnership of Western Europe was a possible card to play in the geopolitical game to contain the Soviet Union. China's reform and opening up after the Third Plenary Session of the 11th Central Committee of the Communist Party of China further paved the way to reach other agreements with the EC; in 1985, both sides signed the EC-China Trade and Economic Cooperation Agreement.[3] The 1985 agreement remains the main legal framework for the relations between

---

[2] Kay Möller puts it this way: "Beijing had entered into an anti-soviet partnership with Washington in 1971/1972 and the EC in 1970 had launched European Political Cooperation (EPC) as the point of departure for a future Common Foreign and Security Policy (CFSP). The role of the European Parliament (EP) had been strengthened in 1974 with the first direct elections scheduled for 1979. Also in 1974, EC heads of state and government had agreed henceforth to convene as the European Council, a *de facto* executive. The EC Commission was authorized to collect its own revenues and to advance into new areas of cooperation such as common trade policies." See Möller, K. (2002). Diplomatic relations and mutual strategic perceptions: China and the European Union. *China Quarterly*, No. 169, pp. 10–32.

[3] Agreement on Trade and Economic Cooperation between the European Economic Community and the People's Republic of China. The Agreement is composed of four chapters (Trade Cooperation, Economic Cooperation, Joint Committee and Final Provisions). See Appendix 1.

the two. In May 1988, the EC Council decided to establish a delegation to China.

The first period was a time when economic cooperation, though at a very low level, was the predominant focus (to a certain extent, it remains so). In this early period, China and Europe were not connected by any grand joint design, but rather by a peripheral consequence of the more central geopolitical phenomena.

The Second Period: From 1989 to 1995

The steady development of bilateral relations was interrupted by the 3–4 June 1989 Tiananmen Incident in Beijing, which saw the beginning of civilization conflicts and the second period in China-European relations, characterized by isolation. Europe, like other major international partners of China, reacted with a range of sanctions. On 7 June 1989, the twelve members of the EU at the time took the decision to suspend economic and cultural relations with China. Since 1990, the EU has sponsored resolutions critical of China at the United Nations Commission on Human Rights sessions held in Geneva. The ensuing end of the Cold War, marked by the collapse of communist regimes in Eastern Europe and the Soviet Union, strengthened this stance of the Europeans.

The second period was a time of transition. Both sides needed time to address and manage the consequences of the end of the Cold War and to formulate more defined policies. It must be noted that the Chinese launched decisive reforms to open up their economy to trade, as well as to restructure the industrial and agricultural sectors during this period. This was especially true from 1992 onwards, when China undertook enormous trade and foreign direct investment (FDI) liberalization — followed by another big dose of liberalization in line with its efforts to join the World Trade Organization (WTO). For the Europeans, however, the importance of China's unilateral liberalization was only to be realized at the end of this period.

The Third Period: From 1995 Up to Now

The third period is characterized by a common EU policy toward China. The EU, for the first time, published "A Long Term Policy for Europe-China Relations" in 1995. On the European side, this document saw the beginning of a real, concrete European policy toward China.

During this period, the EU has seen the opportunity to engage in a rising China for the purpose of realizing its dream of a wider Europe and, perhaps, of counterbalancing the US. In this respect, the EU promulgated strategic relations with China in 2003 with the issuance of the Communication "Building a Comprehensive Partnership with China". The EU's policy paper highlighted China as one of the EU's major strategic partners and the EU-China relationship to be a maturing partnership.[4]

II. Current Trade Relations between China and the EU

The EU and China have the world's second most important trade-and-investment relationship (after the transatlantic relationship). The EU is China's biggest trading partner, ahead of the US and Japan, accounting for 20% of Chinese exports. China is the EU's second biggest trading partner and its biggest source of goods imports.[5] European multinationals have poured investments into China[6] and are prominent in East-Asian supply chains (in which China is usually the location of the last assembly stage before finished products are exported back to the West).

Recent years have seen a dramatic increase in trade between China and the EU, an increase of about 20% per annum in recent years (17% in 2007). This brings us to the question: what exactly is the driving force behind China-EU trade relations?

The most important factor for China-EU trade is the mutual benefits based on the economic complementarity, which serves as the foundation of the trade relation between China and the EU. Indeed, China-EU trade relations are determined by the relative economic performance of both sides, by the degree of complementarity and by mutual benefits. Undoubtedly, China and the EU are highly complementary in an economical sense.

---

[4] EU (2003). *A Maturing Partnership — Shared Interests and Challenges in EU-China Relations.* http://eur-lex.europa.eu/LexUriServ/LexUriServ.do?uri=COM:2003:0533:FIN:EN:PDF (last accessed September 30, 2011).

[5] EU goods imports from China in 2008: €247.6 billion and EU goods exports to China 2008: €78.4 billion, some way ahead of the US and with 16% of the EU market in 2007.

[6] EU FDI stock in China was €32.7 billion in 2006, representing 8% of total FDI stock in China. EU FDI to China was €6 billion in 2006, compared with €2.1 billion of Chinese FDI to the EU. http://ec.europa.eu/trade/issues/bilateral/countries/china/index_en.html. (last accessed September 30, 2011)

China, with a large population, has an abundant and cheap workforce. The Chinese economy has developed rapidly and steadily as witnessed by the world, and its market potential is enormous. However, China lags far behind the EU in terms of the levels of economic and technological development. China's competitive advantage, therefore, rests on labor-intensive products; while the EU's competitive advantage rests on technology-intensive and capital-intensive products. China is mainly exporting light industry goods with low technological content to the EU, and importing machines, equipment, and so on from the EU. Both China and the EU can gain by strengthening this sort of trade linkage. China's rapid economic development in the past thirty years has provided an impetus for and has had a significant impact upon China-EU trade relations. Moreover, the export-oriented strategy that China has pursued for its economic development, which has been given top priority and has preoccupied the leadership since 1978, has reinforced trade relations between China and the EU.

As China and the EU's preferences and interests in developing their bilateral trade relations are part of the broader picture of bilateral relations which integrate security concerns, political strategy, cultural interests and economic gains, China-EU trade relations are set within a favorable political environment. Yet there are some obstacles to the bilateral trade relation that cannot be overlooked.

In fact, it should be noted that such deep trade relations have also led inexorably to commercial and political tensions between the two sides in the new global economic landscape.

III. China and the EU in the New Global Economic Landscape

Any portrait of the global economic landscape cannot be true without a focus on the EU. For hundreds of years, it has occupied the centre stage of the world alone or with the United States. There is no denying that the EU is a highly developed industrialized region, with hundreds of years of industrialization history. The EU is currently the world's second largest single market and accounts for 40% of international trade (including the trade among EU member states).[7] The EU is the world's prime source of FDI outflows as well.

---

[7] EC Delegation in Beijing. http://www.delchn.cec.eu.int/cn/eu_guide/Trade_Relations_Multilateral.htm (last accessed June 30, 2008).

However, the new economic landscape of the globe is also characterized by the rise of China. Since the start of economic reform 30 years ago, the Chinese economy has indeed achieved spectacular performance, growing at an average annual rate of 9.6%. Converted into US dollars at the current exchange rate, China's total GDP in 2010 reached US$5.87 trillion, making it the world's second largest economy after the US.[8] In terms of purchasing power parity (PPP) GDP, China had already been the world's second largest economy after the US for many years.

During the past three decades, the Chinese economy has also been radically transformed from a closed system based on self-reliance to one that is actively participating in the global economic system by way of trade and investment. China's exports have indeed been growing very rapidly, averaging 16% a year since 1978 and over 20% since 2001, rising from US$9.8 billion in 1978 to US$1.2 trillion in 2009, i.e., a 120-fold increase. Since 2009, China has become the world's largest exporting country,[9] and has been the world's second largest recipient of FDI since the early 1990s. By the end of 2007, China had attracted a total of US$7,000 billion in FDI. Not surprisingly, over 80% of the world's largest Fortune 500 companies have established offices in China. Although its trade proportion in international trade currently lags behind that of the EU as a whole, China is already the world's largest trading country and the second largest recipient of FDI after the US.[10]

China's growing political and economic weight has increased its importance in the international arena. By its sheer size, China's level of production, consumption, imports and exports carry significant worldwide ramifications. China's large-scale manufacturing of a wide range of industrial products, as well as its huge labor supply, has substantially brought down the world prices of these products, thus bringing tremendous benefits to consumers globally and competition pressure to the domestic producers of these products. Meanwhile, on account of its massive industrialization, China has become the world's largest consumer of a wide

---

[8] See http://www.bloomberg.com/.../2010.../china-economy-passes-japan-s-in-second- quarter-capping-three-decade-rise.html (last accessed June 30, 2008).

[9] See http://www.cbsnews.com/.../main6078497.shtml (last accessed June 30, 2008).

[10] EU (2001). *EU Strategy towards China: Implementation of the 1998 Communication and Future Steps for a more Effective EU Policy.* http://europa.eu.int/comm/external_relations/china/com01_265.pdf (last accessed June 30, 2008).

range of natural resources and primary commodities from iron cores and aluminum to oil and gas. The rising demand for these resources in recent years has driven up the world's market prices.

According to estimates, China has been responsible for about 50% of the cumulative growth of these economically sensitive commodities. Whether in booms or busts, therefore, the movement of China's economic forces has become a significant factor in the global economy. Various terms, such as 'the world's powerhouse and workshop', have been coined to describe China's influence on the global economy. Despite all of the above, China's external economic impact can be best manifested in its unique pattern of trade balances with its major trade partners.

The EU and China play important roles in Europe and Asia respectively. As the largest developed economy and the fastest-growing developing economy respectively, the EU and China are nations with growing power and influence on international affairs. They are recognized as two important global leaders in today's world and positive participants in the processes of multi-polarizations and economic globalization.

Moreover, as far as bilateral relations are concerned, these two big powers provide mutual inspiration and mutual interaction by their very existence. The EU especially needs to expand and to enhance its presence, including the acquisition of access to more markets in the world, especially in Asia. The EC Communication "Europe and Asia: A Strategic Framework for Enhanced Partnerships" has made clear that "the EU is in need of other markets and China is potentially the biggest".[11] In all these aspects, it is necessary for the EU to obtain support and mutual cooperation from other regions and countries including Asia and China. As for China, the EU remains every bit an important partner and supporter for its ongoing reform process and its integration with the global economy. In short, both sides have a significant stake in each other's development.

IV. The Evolving Bilateral Legal Framework for China-EU Trade Relations

The conduct of trade relations raises many questions which involve legal as well as economic and political factors. When dealing with trade relations,

---

[11] EU (2001). *Europe and Asia: A Strategic Framework for Enhanced Partnerships.* http://ec. europa.eu/development/icenter/repository/strategy_asia_2001_en.pdf (last accessed September 30, 2011).

one must bear in mind the interaction among these factors. While attention is focused on the economic and political factors, the legal aspects of trade relations are often overlooked. In fact, it is through the legal instrument that the trade-related economic and political policies are implemented, and perhaps more importantly, it is the legal instrument that creates a framework for trade policy formulation.

In theory, each state is free to adopt its own trade policy towards another state. In practice, the existing international obligations may place constraints on this otherwise unfettered freedom. Thus, in regulating trade relations with other states, governments are constrained in their policy choices by international rules.

There are currently only two categories of international rules on trade relations between China and the EU. In addition to the WTO agreements at the multinational level, there are the agreements at the bilateral level.

The EU does not have specific trade agreements with its major trading partners among the developed countries like the United States and Japan. Trade issues are handled through the WTO mechanisms, although the EU has many agreements in individual sectors with both countries. However, while the WTO framework also applies to trade between the EU and China, China and the EU have worked together in formulating a series of legal instruments for trade relations between China and the EU since 1975: in 1978, China and the EC signed the "China-EC Trade Agreement" to lay down an institutional framework for the bilateral economic and trade relationships, and the two sides put in place the Joint Committee on Trade Cooperation. This bilateral trade agreement marked a major step forward in China-EU trade relations. The 1978 agreement was replaced by the "Agreement on Trade and Economic Cooperation between the European Economic Community and the People's Republic of China" in 1985. This cooperation agreement stressed mainly the cooperation in the areas of agriculture, energy, science and technology, and personal training.[12]

At the unilateral level, it was the EU that took the initiative in promoting China-EU trade relations. In 1994 the EU began to implement a "New Asia Strategy", and in this context the EU later on formulated a

---

[12] EU (1985). *Agreement on Trade and Economic Cooperation Between the European Economic Community and the People's Republic of China—1985*. http://europa.eu.int/comm/external_relations/china/intro/1985_trade_agreement.htm (last accessed June 30, 2008). See Appendix 1.

policy document towards China,[13] that is, the "Long Term Policy for China-Europe Relations", which was adopted by the European Commission in December 1995. This strategy paper built up the principles of the EU's policy towards China and called on the EU to raise its profile in China.[14] In November 1996, the European Commission put forward "A New Strategy of the EU on China"; on 29 June 1998 the European Commission issued a policy paper on "Building a Comprehensive Partnership with China". It proposed "to engage China further in the international community, to support China's transition to an open society based on the rule of law and the respect for human rights, to integrate China further into the world economy, to make Europe's funding go further and to raise the profile of the EU in China."[15] This document elevated the EU's relationship with China to the level of equal importance with the US, Japan and Russia, unveiling a mature and stable era in China-EU trade relations. On 10 September 2003, the EU published a new policy paper on China, "A Maturing Partnership — Shared Interests and Challenges in EU-China relations". The EU stated in this paper that "both sides have to adapt to a fast moving international scene" and, against that background, "the EU and China have an ever-greater interest to work together as strategic partners to safeguard and promote sustainable development, peace and stability. Interests converge on many international governance issues, notably the importance that both attach to the role of the UN in physical and environmental security".[16] Following this EU policy paper on China, China issued "China's EU Policy paper" on 13 October 2003, which was the first strategic paper on the nation's policy towards the EU. A number of measures for boosting China-EU economic cooperation in the subsequent five years were outlined in this policy paper. The paper also pointed out that "[to] strengthen China-EU relations is an important component of China's foreign policy...China is committed to a long-term, stable and full partnership with the EU...

---

[13] EU (1994). *Towards a New Asia Strategy.* http://europa.eu.int/comm/external_relations/asem/asem_process/com94.htm (last accessed June 30, 2008).

[14] EU (1995). *A Long Term Policy for China-Europe Relations.* http://europa.eu.int/comm/external_relations/china/com_98/index.htm (last accessed June 30, 2008).

[15] EU (1998). *Building a Comprehensive Partnership with China.* http://europa.eu.int/comm/external_relations/china/com_98/index.htm (last accessed June 30, 2008).

[16] See footnote 4.

China desires to promote a sound and steady development of China-EU political relations…deepen China-EU economic cooperation and trade." The issuing of this paper was a further sign of the sound development of China and EU's bilateral trade relations.[17]

The above-mentioned documents serve as the legal and policy framework for China-EU trade relations. The EU's latest official Commission Communication marks something of a watershed. It officially boasted a strategic partnership for the first time.

Since 1995, successive policy declarations on the part of the EU attest to the growing importance of China as a trading partner. This process mirrors similar developments in the trade relations between China and the EU. To an extent, it has also eclipsed the developments in trade relations between either of the two sides and a third party, for the EU has become China's largest trading partner, accounting for about a fifth of its external trade.

In a nutshell, the legal basis for bilateral relations has been the Trade and Cooperation Agreement of 1985, although there have been 7 formal agreements and 24 sectoral and regulatory dialogues on a wide range of issues.[18]

Implications of the Legal Framework for Trade Relations

A legal framework for trade, particularly the agreement that states conclude to regulate the bilateral trade, is generally trade-conducive. Moreover, bilateral agreements are generally in a better position than multilateral agreements to address the concerns of the states concerned.

However, with regard to the existing bilateral trade agreements between China and the EU, a close look at some of them, particularly the Agreement on Trade and Economic Cooperation of 1985, the founding stone of the bilateral trade relationship, will reveal that the trade agreements are not better equipped than multilateral agreements to promote trade liberalization. The Agreement is not yet in a position to constrain the trade policy options of either side, thus leading to prospective trade disputes between the two sides.

---

[17] Ministry of Foreign Affairs of the People's Republic of China (2003). China's EU Policy Paper. http://www.fmprc.gov.cn/eng/topics/ceupp/t27708.htm (last accessed October 10, 2011). See also Appendix 2.

[18] http://ec.europa.eu/external_relations/china/index_en.htm (last accessed September 30, 2011).

For example, the provisions of the trade agreement are in fact subject to the whims of "their respective existing laws and regulations".[19] Strictly speaking, the language of the Agreement suggests that the contracting parties are not legally obligated to liberalize their respective trade policy but only to "confirm their determination" to do so.[20] Therefore, the Agreement is by all means a soft one, which opens the door to lax enforcement of itself. Moreover, the agreement was designed to promote economic cooperation as well as trade. It certainly failed to contemplate the problems that would arise in the course of the bilateral trade relationship, and thus it is not in a position to address the problems such as trade deficit, currency revaluation, non-market economy status and the surmounting use of trade defense instruments. When it comes to the settlement of trade disputes, the Agreement does not help a lot. All that the Agreement does in connection with dispute settlement is to have in place a Joint Committee[21] which serves the purpose of settling disputes arising from the implementation of the Agreement. However, no procedures and rules were set forth in the Agreement to facilitate the settlement of disputes.

In fact, the trade agreements are often used to provide ammunition for the otherwise justified trade defense instruments. Use of trade defense instruments in this context often gives rise to trade disputes. In these

---

[19] Article 1 of the Agreement reads "[t]he two Contracting Parties will endeavor, within the framework of their respective existing laws and regulations, and in accordance with the principles of equality and mutual advantage:

— to promote and intensify trade between them;

— to encourage the steady expansion of economic cooperation". See also Appendix 1.

[20] Article 2 of the Agreement provides that "[t]he two Contracting Parties confirm their determination:

(a) to take all appropriate measures to create favorable conditions for trade between them;

(b) to do their utmost to improve the structure of their trade in order to diversify it further;

(c) to examine, each for its own part and in a spirit of goodwill, any suggestions made by the other Party, in particular in the Joint Committee, for the purpose of facilitating trade between them". See also Appendix 1.

[21] The Joint Committee comprising representatives of the European Economic Community on the one hand and representatives of the People's Republic of China on the other is tasked to "monitor and examine the functioning of this Agreement" and to "to examine any questions that may arise in the implementation of this Agreement", among others.

connections, the regulation of the trade issues between China and the EU rest primarily on the WTO agreements.

China and the EU are now negotiating a new Partnership and Cooperation Agreement (PCA), which will update and expand bilateral cooperation since 1985. The EU intends for the PCA to cover political and economic issues, including its non-trade objectives of democracy, human rights, the rule of law, sustainable development, climate change, and labor and environmental standards. Its trade-and-investment priorities for the PCA include: better enforcement of IPRs; mutual recognition of geographical indicators; WTO-plus commitments on services and investment; lower non-tariff barriers to trade (NTBs) and subsidies; more transparent and open government procurement; improved norms and standards; and better functioning of the legal regime.[22] The PCA, when completed, will result in an upgrade of the original 1985 Trade and Cooperation Agreement, covering a wider range of issues, in line with a deeper and more comprehensive twenty-first century relationship.

A China-EU High Level Trade and Economic Dialogue (HLTED) was launched in April 2008, in imitation of the China-US Strategic Economic Dialogue (SED). This attempted 'hardening' of bilateral economic relations is benign. Granted, China-EU relations do not yet suffer from the shrill, China-bashing rhetoric found in the US. But there are pressures on EU policy to head in a more confrontational direction. In-built EU protectionism against China, and Chinese protectionism and foot-dragging on reforms, can be mutually reinforcing. Hence the imperative to bolster the institutional framework for bilateral economic relations — to go beyond low-key, low-level, inconclusive regulatory dialogues and set-piece, photo-op annual summitry. What should be done?

V. Concluding Remarks

China and the EU are both major players in international trade and very close interaction at all levels on trade issues is in place. Both Chinese and EU policy makers are fully aware of the benefits of free and open markets. Although China-EU relations have been developing rapidly in the last three decades, there is still untapped potential for improved trade relations

---

[22] Zeng, L. (2009). A preliminary perspective of negotiations of EU-China PCA: A new bottle carrying old wine or new wine or both? *European Law Journal*, 15(1), pp. 121–141.

between these two countries. For instance, China shared only 8.4% of the EU's total imports and 18.8% of the EU's total exports in 2010.[23] The EU still exports more to the 7.5 million people who live in Switzerland than to the 1.3 billion people who live in China.

To further develop trade potential between China and the EU, it is necessary to improve mutual cooperation. Both sides tend to seek consensus-oriented solutions in order to avoid conflict — a path which implies lengthy co-ordination before decisions can be taken. Nevertheless, it is imperative to tackle existing problems in bilateral trade relations by institutionalizing bilateral trade cooperation.

A 'strategic partnership' must be based on the acceptance of the principle that both parties have common problems which require common solutions. As both parties negotiate the PCA, they should identify priority issues for careful scrutiny and discussion; issues that are amenable to mutually beneficial bargains.

---

[23] See http://trade.ec.europa.eu/doclib/html/113366.htm (last accessed September 30, 2011).

CHAPTER 2

TRADE DISPUTES BETWEEN CHINA AND THE EU

Recent years have witnessed a dramatic increase of trade between China and the EU. Developing alongside the robust China-EU trade relations were vigorous EU trade measures to pressurize China to trade fairly, respect intellectual property rights and meet its WTO obligations, as well as China's angry response to these measures. Moreover, China-EU trade relations are being overshadowed by prospective disputes which may arise anytime if the concerns of both parties, whether trade related or otherwise, are not addressed in a timely and appropriate manner.

I. Why Trade Disputes Arise between China and the EU

By its nature, trade between states is a game of give and take. In the view of neo-realists, trade disputes between states are merely a "relative gains" problem.[1] If states are more concerned about relative gains than absolute gains, this will limit their willingness to cooperate.[2] As things stand, China is unlikely to make most of these concessions, while the EU seems unready to concede anything major to China. In view of this, trade disputes are probable in such high-pressure bilateral trade relations.

Traditionally, the EU has had a rather liberal trade policy, especially during the years when the internal market was still opening up and integrating. Ironically, as China rises with the help of economic globalization, the EU has become more defensive and inward-looking, particularly since the start of the global economic crisis. Since the internal market is under

---

[1] Marrow, J. D. (1997). When do "relative gains" impede trade? *Journal of Conflict Resolution*, 41(1), 12–37.

[2] Burchill, S. and A. Linklater, eds. (2001). *Theories of International Relations*. 2nd Edition. Houndmills: Palgrave. Chapter 3.

15

stress and deprived of the oxygen of market reforms, trade policy has become more protectionist. That inevitably makes the EU more defensive in its trade with third countries.

II. Robust China-EU Trade Relations Overshadowed by Prospective Disputes

Trade between China and the European Union has been spurred by the liberalization of markets after China's accession to the WTO. While the EU's open market has been a large contributor to China's export-led growth, it has also benefited from the growth of the Chinese market. China is Europe's fastest growing export market (see Figure 1). Indeed, the commitments made by China as a result of its accession to the WTO have secured improved access for EU firms to China's markets. Many import tariffs and other non-tariff barriers have been sharply and permanently lifted.

However, hidden behind such outwardly robust China-EU trade relations are the grave concerns of both sides. From time to time, the EU blames China for engaging in unfair trading practices, including failure to live up to its WTO commitments, the slow pace of currency revaluation, and intellectual property infringements. In turn, China has its own complaints against the EU, which can be characterized either as embracing a protectionist approach to trade remedies such as anti-dumping and technical barriers, or politicizing trade issues. In response to China's increasingly assertive trade practices, the EU has begun treating China as a mature WTO member and is likely to push China harder to achieve its own

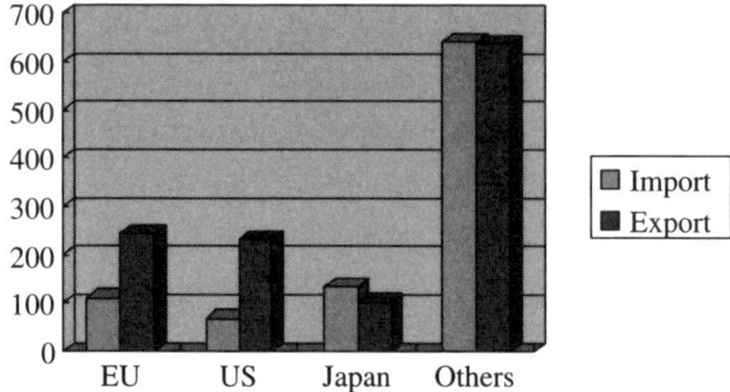

Figure 1:   China's exports and imports in 2007 (billions of US dollars).

Source: Chinese Ministry of Commerce statistics, http://ozs.mofcom.gov.cn/accessory/ 200801/1201137340455.xls (last accessed October 10, 2011).

ends, which often leads to an angry response from China, implying more future confrontations and disputes between the two trade giants.

The EU's Concerns

China's WTO compliance

While China has made good progress in implementing measures to meet its WTO commitments, there are still outstanding problems. Barriers to trade in China are estimated to cost EU businesses €20 billion in lost trade opportunities every year. This amount is equivalent to New Zealand's total imports, or Bulgaria's total GDP. It represents one-third of current EU exports to China. Market impediments are generally held responsible for the EU's trade deficit.

The EU's surging trade deficit also highlights the acuteness of the issue of revaluation of the renminbi. Since July 2005, the renminbi has appreciated 21% in value against the dollar. To the dismay of the EU, during this same period, the renminbi has weakened some 10% against the euro, damaging European competitiveness.

Trade deficit

Though the EU enjoyed a trade surplus with China at the beginning of the 1980s, it is now experiencing a sizeable and widening trade deficit with China. Its trade deficit with China is growing at a rate of €17 million per hour. In 2007, the EU's trade deficit with China was US$134 billion (see Figure 2).

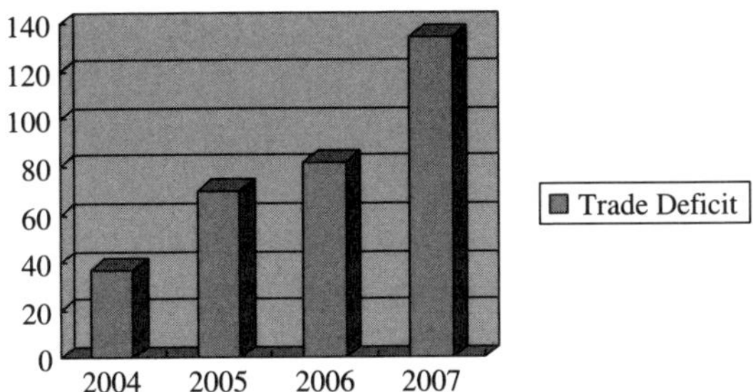

Figure 2:   EU's trade deficit with China (billions of US dollars).

Source: Chinese Ministry of Commerce statistics, http://ozs.mofcom.gov.cn/date/date.html?878713802=201021409.

Although a large consumer market is developing in China, as earlier mentioned, the EU still exports more to the 7.5 million people who live in Switzerland than to the 1.3 billion people who live in China.

It is natural for a high-cost developed economy to run a deficit with a low-cost developing economy; it is the size of the deficit, and the fact that it is rising that causes concern. In the eyes of protectionists, the deficit reflects considerable access problems that EU businesses face in the Chinese market. Under pressure with regard to the trade deficit, the European objective is to either reduce Chinese imports or increase European exports to China. While the former is tantamount to a protectionist reaction, which will certainly lead to contention with China, the latter requires unfettered market access in China. Once again, this is a bone of contention as Beijing insists that market access exists, while European companies insist otherwise.

Renminbi revaluation

It has long been argued that the renminbi was undervalued against the US dollar by approximately 25%–40%. There has been a growing chorus that this fixed valuation has unfairly helped China to gain shares in global markets, and that the value of the renminbi should therefore be raised or immediately floated to let market forces decide its value. To critics, China's exchange rate policy allows Chinese firms to export goods to the EU at artificially low prices, resulting in job losses in the EU.

However, Chinese processing industries will be unhappy to see a sharp rise in the value of the renminbi, which would eat into a substantial part of their small profits from the export market. China fears that an abrupt switch to a freely floating exchange rate, particularly if accompanied by an abolition of its controls on financial outflows, could trigger capital flight and jeopardize its economy in view of the fragility of its banking system. Accordingly, mounting EU and US pressure has induced only slight changes in the Chinese exchange rate regime. Since July 2005, the renminbi has appreciated in value against the dollar, but has weakened some 10% against the euro. Economists argued that the problem is with the weak dollar and not the strong renminbi, so long as the Chinese currency continues to peg itself to the dollar.

Critics contend that China's policies amount to market-distorting currency manipulation. For the US and possibly for the EU, the RMB practices amount to the equivalent of a subsidy to exports and a tariff on imports that would violate WTO rules if imposed directly. The US therefore suggests that the RMB must appreciate approximately 40% against the dollar to correct current 'global imbalances'. It is likely that the EU will join the concerted efforts against the Chinese currency practices.

The issues of trade imbalance and restricted market access are the EU's primary concerns, and if not addressed or improperly addressed, may damage trade relations between China and the EU.

China's Concerns

Major target of anti-dumping measures

China is the primary target of the EU's trade defense instruments, including anti-dumping policies, countervailing safeguard measures and other trade remedies. The EU has accused China of overproduction and dumping key sensitive products like steel and textiles, and has responded with anti-dumping measures under both EC regulations and the WTO Anti-dumping Agreements. In fact, China is the biggest target of EC anti-dumping investigations. The EU even extends its anti-dumping duty against Chinese products produced in other customs territories such as Macau. Although covering less than 2% of Chinese trade, the 41 EC anti-dumping measures currently in place against Chinese imports have had a severe impact on Chinese exporters.

Moreover, under existing EC regulations on anti-dumping, Chinese imports are in an even more disadvantaged position, since the built-in mechanism in the EC regulations is likely to be manipulated. The 'analogy country' method, for example, is widely used by the EC to calculate the dumping margin in anti-dumping cases. This practice is discriminative in nature and ignores the comparative advantage of Chinese enterprises.

China is concerned with the EC using the 'analogy country' methodology. The pleas of Chinese enterprises over the choice of the methodology are usually not accepted by the EC. It is not clear whether the criteria for determining an 'analogy country' relates to the level of development of the countries concerned, the respective production processes, the comparability of the products, or the comparability of the respective industries. The fact that China remains the primary target, together with the manipulative practices in anti-dumping, has caused great concern among Chinese companies.

China-specific 'non-market economy' denomination

Closely related to the EU's anti-dumping and countervailing measures is China's non-market economy (NME) status. When it comes to anti-dumping and countervailing measures, China is currently treated as an economy in transition, meaning that prices and costs are assumed to be influenced by the state. Other countries can use prices of third-country markets as benchmarks to compare domestic prices to determine if China is dumping or over-subsidizing products.

If China gains ME recognition, investigating authorities will have to use prices and costs reported by the individual companies under investigation, therefore boosting China's ability to fight anti-dumping charges. In this regard, the EU is using the ME denomination as the most powerful instrument available to exert leverage over China. However, in a report on 28 June 2008, the EC clearly concluded that China is not yet a "market economy". Rather, it listed four conditions for China to fulfill: reduce state interference in firms; increase the level of compliance with accounting law; ensure equal treatment under bankruptcy law and respect for property and IPRs; and apply market rules in the banking sector. The fact that the conditions are quite subjective shows that the EC is reluctant to forgo the leverage that can be used to punish China for non-compliance or induce China to give more concessions. China is clearly resentful of such treatment.

Textiles-related trade defense instruments specifically against Chinese products

Before the termination of the Agreement on Textiles and Clothing (ATC) at the end of 2005, China expected the EU as well as the US to eliminate all existing restrictions on the import of textiles and clothing products from 1 January 2005, in accordance with the requirement of the ATC. However, China noticed with concern that the EU was making increasing use of trade remedies. Indeed, the EC had in place product-specific safeguards targeted at textiles and clothing products, fully integrating these safeguards into normal GATT rules and disciplinary measures in order to take full advantage of China's new commitments to the WTO. China threatened to retaliate against these measures.

To avoid an imminent trade war, both China and the EU were forced to negotiate and reach an agreement which could be rightfully referred to as a 'voluntary restraint arrangement' on the part of China. In the years that followed, the agreement cooled the dispute on Chinese textile exports. As quotas in the 2005 bilateral textiles and clothing agreement expired at the end of 2008, textile and clothing trade disputes are certain to continue for another decade or longer after this, which will test the patience of the industries concerned as well as that of the governments of the EU and China. Should disputes escalate, it is unknown whether the Chinese government will bow to pressure to acquiesce to the new voluntary restraint arrangement for textile exports.

Complicated EC technical/SPS standards/environment criteria

The EU is famous for its great number of stringent and sophisticated technical regulations and standards for consumer products and food. These were ostensibly drawn up for the purpose of protecting human health and life, as well as consumers' interests. However, inappropriate application of these regulations leads to trade protectionism, which exerts a negative influence on EU-bound Chinese exports that are subjected to no or less sophisticated standards in China. These standards, in reality, are green barriers.

Chinese firms are often unprepared for these mounting regulations and standards which are subject to frequent revision. This has caused resentment to grow. Moreover, EC standards affecting Chinese imports are either complex or opaque, and to the Chinese, the EC's standards and their implementation are not necessarily based on empirical data. About half of the products withdrawn from the European market because of consumer faults come from China.

Abuse of trade defense instruments against imports from China

There have been cases where the EU has been found to abuse trade defense instruments to target imports from China. On one occasion, China accused the EU of adopting double standards towards imports of Chinese products. When Chinese firms sold coke in the European market at lower prices, they were charged for dumping and had to pay an anti-dumping levy in 2003, but when the Chinese government restricted coke exports for environmental reasons in 2005, the EC threatened to bring the case to the WTO. This was sheer evidence of double standards.

More alarming to China is the EU's inclination to apply two or more trade measures simultaneously. For example, European firms and the EC used intellectual property rights protection and anti-dumping measures against Chinese imports. A typical example is the import of China-made DVDs players and DVD discs. When Chinese manufacturers of DVD players were accused of intellectual property rights infringement, the EC concurrently launched anti-dumping investigations against Chinese DVD discs in August 2005.

Arms sales embargo

Last but not least important is China's resentment towards the EU's arms embargo that has been in place since the 1989 Tiananmen incident. The issue is more about politics than about trade. However, China sees it as a testing ground for the strategic partnership, which has certainly influenced China-EU relations and the mutual trust between the two parties that is crucial to maintaining smooth trade relations. Moreover, the EU's maintenance of the arms sales embargo could occasionally trigger an irrational Chinese response to trade issues and disputes.

III. A Comparison with Trade Disputes between China and the US

In this regard, it is useful to make a comparison between China-EU trade disputes and China-US trade disputes.

A glance at trade disputes between China and the US will show that both the EU and the US share the same or similar concerns in their trade relations with China. Over the past decade, the widening US-China trade deficit has been the focal point of bilateral relations, and has often been portrayed as a cause for overall US current account imbalances. However, real public concerns are rooted in the perceived economic threat of competition from Chinese imports.

Perceptions of China by the US and the EU are similar with regard to unfair competition from imports, illegal export subsides, lax enforcement of intellectual property rights, restricted market access, and an undervalued national currency.[3]

---

[3] Hufbauer, G. C., Y. Wong, and K. Sheth (2006). *US-China Trade Disputes: Rising Tide, Rising Stakes.* The Peterson Institute for International Economics, August, pp. 4–10.

These concerns have fueled calls for legislation to prevent unfair practices. In February 2005, the US Senate passed the Byrd Amendment, encouraging American companies to file anti-dumping investigation applications by awarding the revenue collected from the resultant tariffs to litigating companies. Other specifically anti-China legislation proposed since then includes a bill declaring exchange rate protection to be an illegal subsidy for which US firms can seek compensation.[4]

However, compared with China-EU commercial disputes, the trade disputes between China and the US are even more prominent. In fact China-US trade disputes occurred before China-EU disputes,[5] and the intensity has never abated as the Chinese economy boomed and the US economy slumped in the past decade.

Three political and economic factors seem to have a bearing on the occurrence and handling of prospective trade disputes with China. Firstly, the EU has been seen to adopt a distinct attitude towards China's rise. The US sees China as a competitor, and is somewhat intolerant of China's rise. Indeed, in the US, the aversion to the prospect of a strong prosperous China under an authoritarian state is more palpable than in the EU. The EU and China have agreed to a comprehensive strategic partnership, while the US views China as a stakeholder at best. The political tolerance on the EU side, cemented in the "Comprehensive Strategic Partnership",[6] is supposed to soften and moderate EU complaints.

Secondly, the EU has also been found to take a different approach toward managing disputes, and pressing China towards a pre-determined goal. Compared with the more assertive stance of the US, the EU's approach is much softer. It either adopts a proactive approach or is satisfied with silently following a provocative US. However, an internal document was reported to be the harbinger of an EC attempt to align with the US to pressurize China.

---

[4] *Ibid.*, p. 23.

[5] The early 1990s saw frequent eruptions of Sino-American disputes over intellectual property rights. See Kong, Q. (2003). Intellectual property rights protection in Post-WTO China, still an incurable blight on Sino-US trade relations? *Issues & Studies*, 38(3), pp. 59–79.

[6] In a Joint Statement of the 9th EU-China Summit on 9 September 2006, both parties announced the existence of a comprehensive strategic partnership between them. Since January 2007, China and EU started negotiating a comprehensive Partnership and Cooperation Agreement (PCA).

Thirdly, although the EU is a single customs union with a single trade policy and tariff, it takes time to build consensus among its 27 members. It has been difficult for the EU to agree on a single policy toward China; each member state has its own history of dealing with China, and some of them have competing economic interests. Therefore, the EU might not be as efficient as the US in dealing with China.

CHAPTER 3

AN EMPIRICAL STUDY OF TRADE DEFENSE INSTRUMENTS AND THEIR USES

I. Introduction

It should be noted that trade defense instruments are regarded as technical instruments, which should be judged on their own merits. Nevertheless, a thorough assessment of the trade defense instruments of both China and the EU must be further based on the merits of their approaches to the use of these instruments. With this in mind, one needs to look into the contexts of trade disputes, and closely examine how trade defense instruments operate.

In terms of the absolute number of definitive measures, the EU has been one of the biggest users of anti-dumping measures in the global economy since the World Trade Organisation (WTO) was founded in 1995. Among the biggest targets of the EU's anti-dumping measures is China. Although the EU cut its anti-dumping cases against other countries by a third between 2002–2006 compared with the 1995–2001 period, the number of anti-dumping cases against China remained constant up to 2006 (roughly six cases a year). Every year, Chinese companies become involved in newly launched EU anti-dumping investigations. Moreover, the number of anti-dumping cases per billion euros of EU imports also shows substantial discrimination against China, with a figure for China twice as high as that for the rest of the world.[1] Meanwhile China has also increasingly used its own trade defense instruments against imports of products from its European trade partners. This practice alone may have caused both parties to harbor discontent against each other with regard to trade relations,

---

[1] See Messerlin, P. and J. Wang (2008). *The EU Trade Policy towards China*, available at http://www.gem.sciences-po.fr/content/publications/pdf/Messerlin_wang_EUchina_EN20022008.pdf (last accessed June 30, 2008).

25

especially when the use of trade defense instruments is not in line with WTO agreements.

It has been observed that the trade defense instruments are sometimes used by both parties for protectionist purposes. For example, anti-dumping remedies — as a trade defense instrument — have been transformed from a legitimate shield against unfair practices into a distortionary intervention in the marketplace, with both projectionist consequence. Ironically, anti-dumping remedies have sometimes been used as leverage to compel trade partners to use trade defense instruments in a correct and responsible way. This chapter provides an overview of both China's and the EU's trade defense instruments by dissecting the anti-dumping remedies of both parties and revealing their ramifications.

In this regard, case studies will shed light on how trade disputes between China and the EU have festered and escalated amid the use of trade defense instruments. Of the many disputes that have strained trade relations between China and the EU, perhaps the two most revealing case studies to examine would be light bulbs and leather shoes.

Before conducting an analysis and discussion on the anti-dumping practices of both the EU and China, it is useful to set forth three criteria by which to make this assessment. In light of this, anti-dumping remedies of both the EU and China are approached from the standpoints of consistency with the WTO, effectiveness (suggesting ways in which anti-dumping remedies could be strengthened consistently with WTO obligations) and desirability (identifying areas in which added detail might be desirable for the benefit of the public and the administering authority).

II. How Trade Disputes are Fermented Amid the Use of Trade Defense Instruments

An Overview of EU Trade Defense Instruments[2]

Like most other importing economies, the EU has a system of trade defense instruments. These instruments — anti-dumping, anti-subsidy and safeguard measures — are designed to defend European producers against

---

[2] For a systematic study of how the EU's trade defense instruments are used, see Communication from the Commission of 6 December 2006. Global Europe: Europe's Trade Defense Instruments in a Changing Global Economy — A Green Paper for Public Consultation [COM(2006) 763 final].

unfairly traded or subsidized imports, as well as against dramatic shifts in trade flows insofar as these are harmful to the EU economy. In other words, trade defense instruments are supposed to serve as legitimate and essential instruments against unfair trade practices or against a sudden unexpected surge of imports, which causes, or threatens to cause, serious damage to the EU economy. In particular, anti-dumping and anti-subsidy measures contribute to the restoration and promotion of fair competition.

Nevertheless, trade defense instruments are an EC policy area that provokes strong passions and where people have strong views. A wide range of views exist on trade defense instruments, particularly on anti-dumping measures. At one end of the spectrum, some people see trade defense instruments as a critical defense against unfair trade practices and distortions to trade. On the other hand, others think that the use of trade defense instruments can only be justified on rare occasions and, with this in mind, propose that trade defense instruments should be abolished. In this way, it is perhaps unique of all EC policy areas. Given this, an objective evaluation of this policy area may be helpful with regard to highlighting policy issues in the EU's trade defense instruments and in understanding the occurrence of trade disputes between the EU and China in this area.

The EC has traditionally been reluctant to impose safeguard measures on third-world country exports of industrial products. At first sight, safeguard measures seem less attractive in terms of relief than anti-dumping duties and countervailing duties: quotas do not directly affect the prices charged for imported products (but raise domestic prices), which may continue to hurt EC industries, and there are stricter time limits. In addition, under the WTO rules, the EC must offer compensation to the main WTO suppliers affected by the protective measures.[3] Lastly, unlike anti-dumping and anti-subsidy measures, safeguards target fair trade and therefore amount to an admission by domestic industries that they cannot compete fairly with traded imports. Thus, safeguards have traditionally been viewed as an instrument for 'wimps'. For these reasons, safeguard actions were not popular with EC member states and industries, and few such cases were brought up in the past. Using this moral high ground, the EC has gone on the offensive since 1995, challenging safeguard measures imposed by other WTO members, including Korea, Argentina and, repeatedly, the US, in the WTO.

---

[3] This must take place either immediately, or after three years if the measure is the result of an absolute increase in imports that conforms with the WTO rules.

Almost all trade defense actions taken by the EU against Chinese products are in the form of anti-dumping measures.[4] This merely reflects the fact that other defense instruments are less 'advantageous' for domestic applicants, that is, they deliver a lower rate of protection than anti-dumping procedures.[5] When it comes to China, the EU has only used the countervailing instrument once in cases involving Chinese companies, partly due to the fact that China is treated as a non-market transition economy. However, the EU has used anti-subsidy measures in conjunction with anti-dumping measures against Chinese products in the EU.[6]

The anti-dumping remedy is embodied in the Council Regulation (EC) No. 384/96 of 22 December 1995 on protection against dumped imports from countries not members of the European Community, which was amended by the Council Regulation (EC) No. 2331/96 of 2 December 1996, No. 905/98 of 27 April 1998, No. 2238/2000 of 9 October 2000, No. 1972/2002 of 5

---

[4] The first EU safeguard measure against China took place when the EC launched a safeguard investigation concerning imports of certain prepared or preserved citrus fruits (namely mandarins, etc.) on 11 July 2003. The EU launched its first anti-subsidy investigation into Chinese products (namely coated papers) on 17 April 2010.

[5] When asked whether the EU makes greater use of anti-subsidy and safeguard instruments alongside its anti-dumping actions, the EC explained, *inter alia*, why the trade defense actions have primarily consisted of anti-dumping measures, and why it did not take the initiative to institute anti-subsidy and safeguard measures: Anti-dumping and safeguards investigations should be launched on the basis of a complaint introduced by the European sector concerned. Anti-subsidy investigations could be initiated by the European Commission on its own initiative provided that prior informal contacts took place with the sector in question.

When an illegal subsidy is not specifically linked to one sector but is applied in a horizontal way, the European Commission should consider launching a complaint in the WTO against this unfair trade practice.

As far as safeguards are concerned, these are instruments of 'last resort' that should be used with care as they could lead to retaliatory measures from the third-world country, even if the initial measures are intended to limit imports which increase in such a way that cause or risk causing serious damage to domestic producers.

[6] The EU launched an anti-dumping investigation into imports of Chinese coated fine paper in February 2010, followed by an anti-subsidy investigation two months later. On 14 May 2011, it decided to impose its first-ever anti-subsidy and anti-dumping duties on imports from China.

November 2002, No. 461/2004 of 8 March 2004 and No. 2117/2005 of 21 December 2005 (hereinafter referred to as anti-dumping rules).[7]

An Overview of the EU's Anti-dumping Remedies

Anti-dumping rules are the most utilized trade defense instrument in the EU. Anti-dumping measures address the import of goods that are priced in foreign markets at less than their normal value in the home market — usually as a result of the lack of competition and/or state interference in the production process that allows an exporter to artificially lower the cost of an export. Typical examples of distortions leading to dumping include: significant tariff and non-tariff barriers, insufficient enforcement of competition rules, export tax breaks, and artificially low raw material and/or energy prices. When an investigation shows that these imports are harming domestic producers, anti-dumping rules allow for remedial measures to address the injury. Normally this takes the form of a duty being imposed on the dumped import.

The rationale for anti-dumping measures has traditionally been to prevent international price discrimination. Selling in foreign markets at a price lower than in the domestic economy is unfair because it is indicative of trade barriers in the home market; otherwise, arbitrage and the re-importation of domestic goods would eliminate the price differential.

However, an evaluation of China's complaints in the iron and steel fasteners case will show how dissatisfied China was with EU anti-dumping measures. China complained about Article 9(5) of Council Regulation (EC) No. 384/96 (the EC's Basic Anti-dumping Regulation), which provides that in the case of imports from non-market economy countries, the duty shall be specified for the supplying country concerned and not for each supplier, and that an individual duty will only be specified for exporters that demonstrate that they fulfill the criteria listed in that provision. China also accused Article 9(5) of the Basic Anti-dumping Regulation for being inconsistent with the European Communities' obligations under Article XVI(4) of the WTO Agreement, Articles I(1), VI(1), and X(3a) of the GATT 1994, and Articles 6.10, 9.2, 9.3, 9.4, 12.2.2 and 18.4 of the Anti-dumping Agreement. It further charged that the imposition of definitive

---

[7] EU (1995). http://eur-lex.europa.eu/LexUriServ/LexUriServ.do?uri=CONSLEG: 1996R0384: 20051230:EN:PDF (last accessed September 30, 2011).

anti-dumping duties on imports of certain iron or steel fasteners originating in the People's Republic of China was inconsistent with the European Communities' obligations under Articles VI and X(3a) of the GATT 1994, Articles 1, 2.1, 2.2, 2.4, 2.6, 3.1, 3.2, 3.4, 3.5, 4.1, 5.4, 6.1, 6.2, 6.4, 6.5, 6.10, 9.2, 9.4 and 17.6(i) of the Anti-dumping Agreement, Part I, paragraph 15 of China's Protocol of Accession, and Articles 9.3 and 12.2.2 of the Anti-dumping Agreement.[8]

China claimed that the EU acted inconsistently with various procedural obligations in the Anti-dumping Agreement, and with its substantive obligations under the Anti-dumping Agreement, GATT 1994, and the Protocol of Accession through the application of Article 9(5) of the Anti-dumping Regulation in this investigation, as well as decisions and determinations made in the investigation relating to, *inter alia*, the scope of the product, the extent of the domestic industry, the conduct of the injury analysis and the lack of price comparability adjustments made in the calculation of the anti-dumping margin.

The following is an in-depth analysis of the EU's anti-dumping remedies:

(1) *Administering agencies*

It is desirable and more effective if the authority to wield anti-dumping remedies is exclusively granted to an independent body, for this would minimize political interference, with other considerations not linked to the facts of the investigation itself not being taken into account. However, both the Chinese Anti-dumping Regulations and the EU Anti-dumping rules are applied through a responsibility-sharing system among various agencies. On the EU side, the European Commission is responsible for the conduct of anti-dumping investigations, and reserves the right to decide on whether to open investigations in response to industry complaints, as well as conduct reviews during the life of current measures. It may also impose provisional measures.[9] But the European Commission can only propose definitive measures to the Council, where warranted. It is the Council that can decide to impose definitive anti-dumping measures (only requiring a simple majority). Moreover, while anti-dumping is under the purview of the European Commission and

---

[8] WT/DS397/1, G/L/891, G/ADP/D79/1.

[9] The Council may decide to take a different course of action regarding provisional measures.

the European Council, implementation of anti-dumping measures is taken after voting by various committees with member state representation. The bureaucratic entity responsible for advising member states on anti-dumping measures is the Directorate-General of Trade (DG Trade). The community industry can apply to have an anti-dumping investigation begin. DG Trade first investigates the standing of the complainants. If they are found to represent at least 25% of the community industry, the investigation will most likely be conducted. DG Trade will then make a recommendation to the Anti-dumping Advisory Committee, on which each member state has one vote. The Advisory Committee examines the application. If this consultation reveals that the complaint does not contain sufficient evidence to justify initiating a proceeding, the application is rejected. The Anti-dumping Advisory Committee and the Council also play their respective roles in the application of the anti-dumping measures. Where the final outcome of the EC investigation is negative, and where, after consultation, anti-dumping measures are considered unnecessary, and with there being no objection raised within the Advisory Committee, the proceeding is terminated. If there are any objections, the Commission shall immediately submit to the Council a report on the results of the consultation, together with a proposal that the proceeding be terminated. Then the Council shall make the final decision within one month. In the event of an 'expiry review', the Anti-dumping Advisory Committee may reject the Commission's proposal of of an 'expiry review' of the anti-dumping duties in place on imports of foreign products.

The Council and the Anti-dumping Advisory Committee are member-based bodies, and thus are not free from political considerations while making decisions concerning adoption of the EC's proposal, particularly when the interests of a member state are involved.

(2) *Initiation*

Application by the community industry

The community industry is entitled to initiate an anti-dumping complaint against imports from outside the European Union. Article 4(1) of the Regulation defines the 'community industry' as being "[t]he Community producers as a whole of the like products or to those of them whose collective output of the products constitutes a major proportion … of the total Community production of those products." Article 5(4), which determines the grounds on which an investigation can be initiated following the filing of a complaint, defines 'major proportion' as 50%. The same article goes on to say that no investigation shall be initiated on the basis of a complaint where this figure is less than 25%, which allows the Commission to initiate an investigation on behalf of a complaint by representatives of as little as 25% of Community production. The Commission figures state the complainants represent on average 26.7% of Community production. It is open to debate whether this minimum threshold should be significantly increased to more accurately reflect what could be called a 'major proportion', and whether the figure should exclude EU companies that import the product concerned.

In this regard, a thorny and controversial phenomenon is that the European companies which are behind the complaint are also those which have established their businesses in China and imported these products in the first place. It has been established that China-based subsidiaries of European companies are exempted from anti-dumping investigations while Chinese exporters are subject to anti-dumping duties. This is the case with iron or steel fasteners from China. Italy's Agrati and Spain's Celo, which were behind the anti-dumping complaint, were exempted from the duties for the products imported from their subsidiaries in China.[10]

As EU anti-dumping measures are primarily considered part of a 'trade defense' portfolio, consumer interests and non-industry related interests ('community interests') are not emphasized during an investigation. Although it was argued in the anti-dumping investigation for leather shoes from China and Vietnam, that it would not be in the interest of the Community to subject so-called 'children's shoes' to provisional duties, there is no established exclusion of certain product types under community interest considerations.[11] For the EC, particular products cannot *a priori* be excluded from anti-dumping investigations. Likewise, one should not determine in advance which types of products will never pass the community interest test. The exclusion of certain product types due to Community economic interests would set a precedent for mis-classification and fraud with customs codes. Furthermore, it would mean that when it comes to these goods, unfair trade practices can remain unpunished and are in fact acceptable.

---

[10] On 9 November 2007, the EC decided to launch anti-dumping investigations on the imports of iron and steel fasteners originating in China.

[11] See Tietje, C., M. Bickel and K. Nowrot (2006). *Stamping Out Logic and Reason: EU Anti-Dumping Duties on Leather Shoes*, Policy Papers on Transnational Economic Law, No. 21, available at http://telc.jura.uni-halle.de/sites/default/files/telc/Policy-Paper21.pdf (last accessed September 30, 2011).

Initiation of complaints

As for the acceptance or rejection of anti-dumping investigation applications, Article 5(7) of the Anti-dumping Regulations of the EU states that "[a] complaint shall be rejected where there is insufficient evidence of either dumping or of injury to justify proceeding with the case". However, the EC's anti-dumping rules are silent on the question of whether the applicant can re-file applications where according to the EC, previous applications have been shown to be supported by insufficient evidence. It is not unusual to find applicants file official applications, discuss with Commission staff, and re-file them until they meet the requirements necessary to initiate an investigation. The EU seems to fail to prevent complainants from continually filing complaints once an initial attempt has been rejected.[12] It is for this reason that the majority of investigations conclude with the implementation of definitive measures.

Case Studies

(1) Case history

Case 1: Anti-dumping measures on light bulbs

Osram Opto Semiconductor, a German company and a dominant compact fluorescent lamps (CFL) producer in Europe, requested permission to impose anti-dumping duties against Chinese exports in 2001. The EU imposed an anti-dumping tariff of up to 66% on energy-saving light bulbs from China in 2001, which was originally due to expire in July 2006. However, the EU later conducted an expiration review amid requests by the industry to determine whether to prolong the tariffs for another five years. The review period, which lasted 15 months after the expiration, was set to end in October 2007. On 29 August 2007, the EU agreed to a one-year extension of the six-year-old duties. As a compromise, the anti-dumping measures ended automatically after the extension. The China Association of Lighting Industry (CALI) estimates that half of China's energy saving bulb producers went bankrupt immediately (the

---

[12] China has expressed its concerns that the EC fails to examine, with any particular care, any application for the initiation of an anti-dumping investigation where a previous investigation of the same product from China resulted in a negative finding within the 365 days prior to the filing of the application.

number of such producers dropped from 4,000 to around 2,000 in 2001, and further to around 1,400 in 2002).

Case 2: Anti-dumping measures on leather shoes, August 2006

In October 2006, the EU imposed duties of 16.5% and 10% respectively on certain leather shoes imported from China and Vietnam to the European Union. These duties, which were the result of an investigation that found that dumping of these exports from China and Vietnam had led to consequent injury to EU producers, had meant the levying of duties during 2008 amounting to more than 200 million euros. The anti-dumping duties were supposed to last for two years, but in October 2009, the Commission commenced a sunset review in order to clarify if there was a need for further measures or if these measures could be terminated. The review by the Commission concluded with a proposal to prolong the anti-dumping measures for another 15 months. The proposal was later discussed within the anti-dumping advisory committee and at the beginning of January 2010, the Council made the decision as proposed.[13] The application of EU and WTO rules in this highly complex case provoked divisions among EU economic operators and EU member states.

Following the application of anti-dumping duties against China's exports of leather shoes in April 2006, Chinese manufacturers were squeezed by both decreasing orders and by the demand from distributors in the EU to reduce prices, leading to the closure of many smaller enterprises and massive job losses.[14]

(2) *Stakeholders and the community interest test in the use
      of trade defense instruments*

Although both the CFL and leather shoes anti-dumping cases came to a close, they illustrated the most important issues: stakeholders and their interactions in the application of the community interest test, which determines the use of trade defense instruments.

---

[13] It has been established that the Council has almost systematically extended initial measures for indefinite periods.

[14] For example, a Guangdong-based company, which exported 500,000 pairs of shoes to Italy in 2005, was asked (in April 2006) by its Italian distributors to cut the order by half and reduce the price from 25 yuan (US$3) to 21 yuan (US$2.5) a pair. Available at http://english.peopledaily.com.cn/200604/10/eng20060410_257193.html (last accessed September 30, 2011).

Generally speaking, stakeholders in proceedings involving trade defense instruments include exporters, importers and downstream users. However, EU trade defense activities involve more stakeholders, such as member states, community industry, exporters, importers, downstream users, and even environmentalist groups.

In the light bulb case, a wide range of stakeholders were involved: Osram, the Chinese CFL producers, European companies that produce CFL in China, importers and retailers of China-made CFL, downstream users of CFL, environmentalists and member states.

Osram Opto Semiconductor, the German manufacturer of lamps and parts and a unit of the industrial conglomerate Siemens AG, was the initiator of the anti-dumping investigation. Osram is still manufacturing over 50% of its energy-saving lamps in Europe.

The Chinese CFL producers are the targets of these anti-dumping measures. Standing on the same side of the Chinese CFL producers are European companies that produce CFL in China.

The case divided Europe's light bulb makers between those which have production plants in China and those focusing on local production in Europe. While Osram does have factories in China, its CFL production remains focused in Europe. Philips Lighting, Europe's largest lamp and lighting manufacturer, produced energy-saving lamps in the most expensive product segment in Europe, and therefore imports cheap energy-saving lamps from China to supplement its product range in Europe. Although both Osram and Philips have part of their production based in China to reduce costs, Philips has a much larger presence, and imports more than other European companies, to such an extent that it can hardly be classified as a European producer. As Osram has pushed to keep the duties in place, Philips Lighting and other EU producers with their main production facilities in Asia complain that the duties have been squeezing their profit margins. These companies have been fighting their own case at the EU Court of First Instance to have the anti-dumping duties scrapped completely.[15] In a study of the leather shoes case by the National Board of Trade in 2007, it was found that even if shoe manufacturers moved their physical manufacturing outside the Community, the main part of 'added value', in the form of design, research and development and marketing,

---

[15] Philips criticized the EC's decision to extend the anti-dumping duties. "Continuing duties would be a backward, protectionist move to safeguard the short-term interests of one single company".

are done within the Community.[16] A shoe manufactured in China might therefore still be regarded as a 'European' shoe, which means that the EU was introducing anti-dumping measures directed at itself. Thus, these duties and the system itself contradicted European companies' efforts to reap the benefits of globalization, and undermined their own competitiveness.[17]

Importers and retailers of China-made products are downstream users of products in both the light bulb case and the leather shoes case. To some extent, they share the same interest in the anti-dumping case. For them, the tariffs ensured that prices were 'artificially inflated' when the products reached the shops and this depressed demand for energy-saving bulbs and leather shoes. In the light bulbs case, the Foreign Trade Association (FTA), which represents EU importers, was critical of the EC's decision to extend the anti-dumping duties against Chinese CFL.[18]

Environmentalists also have a stake in the case. They criticized the anti-dumping measures as unjustified in the EU's fight against global warming. Since 2002, the market for energy-saving lighting in Europe has changed. While the use of traditional filament bulbs is expected to be gradually reduced in more and more countries,[19] governments are now promoting the use of energy-saving lamps that offer less energy consumption and a longer usage life, in an effort to reduce CO_2 emissions. Without the anti-dumping duties, the price of China-made energy-saving lamps would be about the same as regular light bulbs. This should also please the European

---

[16] See The National Board of Trade (2007). *Adding Value to the European Economy.* http://www.kommers.se/upload/Analysarkiv/Arbetsomr%C3%A5den/EUs%20yttre%20handelspolitik/AddingvaluetotheEuropeaneconomy.pdf (last accessed September 30, 2011).

[17] See the website of the National Board of Trade: http://www.kommers.se/templates/Standard_5657.aspx (last accessed June 30, 2008).

[18] "It is not good for the European industry as some major producers do not want the duties to be extended. Also, it is not good for consumers since the prices are already high because of the duties", FTA spokesman Stuart Newman told Xinhua.

[19] For example, in 2008 the Dutch Minister of the Environment, Jacqueline Kramer, suggested completely phasing out the use of the traditional light bulb in the Netherlands. As the European Union already uses trade defense instruments in a more strict and balanced way than the WTO rules impose (lesser-duty rule, *de minimis*, community interest test, etc.), there is no need for a fundamental review of these instruments. Possible improvements should aim to increase the transparency and predictability of trade defense instruments, but should under no circumstances put into question the legitimacy of the instruments or undermine their efficiency.

environmental lobby, since these lamps increase power efficiencies while reducing electrical product waste. The World Wildlife Fund (WWF) urged the EU to end the duties, arguing that Europe has to rely on imports to meet its demand for low-energy light bulbs, which is instrumental, if not essential, to realizing the bloc's goal of reducing greenhouse gas emissions by 20% by 2020 from 1990 levels. The WWF argued that, "Ending the anti-dumping investigation and allowing imports of Chinese integrated compact fluorescent lamps could contribute to savings of 23 million tons of CO_2 per year, equivalent to 0.5% of EU greenhouse gas emissions".[20]

EU member states are also stakeholders in this case. In the light bulbs case, the Netherlands, UK, Sweden, Denmark, Poland and four other countries have kept up the pressure to reverse the anti-dumping ruling. At the EU anti-dumping committee vote in September 2007 on terminating the anti-dumping measures, some ten members voted in favour while nine voted against, the latter including Germany, France, Hungary and Italy. In the leather shoes case, Sweden forcefully objected (along with eleven other member states) to the introduction of the anti-dumping measures. Sweden questioned if it was in the Community's interest to impose these measures, with the (negative) effects of expected price increases for consumers being among many concerns raised. Sweden estimated that the measures against Chinese and Vietnamese leather shoes would have an adverse and dispro-portionate effect on market participants such as designers, importers, marketers, distributors and retailers, resulting in a significant overall wel-fare loss for the EU as a whole.

Interestingly, within the European Commission, commissioners were also divided over the case. For example, in July 2007 a majority of trade experts in the European Commission decided to support an end to the anti-dumping measures. While Mandelson, the EU's top trade official, shared this position, the EU's Industry Commissioner Guenter Verheugen pressed for a two-year transition period and has expressed concern about job losses at German producer Osram.

As a result, the extension proposal was a result of compromise mainly between Osram and Phillips, between European CFL producers and European producers that produce CFL in China, between European indus-try and importers, retailers and consumers, between European industry and environmentalists, between member states and even between the EU's

---

[20] See World Wildlife Fund (WWF), http://www.wwf.dk/dk/Service/.../WWF.../ EU+consumption+global+pollution (last accessed June 30, 2011).

Trade Commissioner and Industry Commissioner. That perhaps is why the EU Trade Commissioner Mandelson had to admit in a statement that this case has "… shown the complexities of managing anti-dumping rules in a global economy and against the broad range of EU interests".[21]

When examining the community interest, before jumping to the use of trade defense instruments, we need to understand that the community interest test issue is largely brought about by outsourcing by EU producers. As shown in the light bulbs and leather shoes cases, many more EU companies now produce goods outside the EU to export back to the EU, or operate supply chains that stretch beyond the EU market. Although many EU companies still produce light bulbs and leather footwear in the European Union, a significant number of EU companies have outsourced the production of light bulbs and footwear to third-world countries while keeping other parts of their operations in the EU. These changes challenge familiar understandings of what constitutes EU production and the EU's economic interests. Those EU companies that produce light bulbs and leather shoes in China are subject to anti-dumping duties. Moreover, under the existing rules for anti-dumping investigations, only producers that keep their production within the EU are taken into consideration in determining whether the required proportion of Community industry for the case to be initiated has been met. Yet the number of EU companies that are moving elements of their production is growing and these companies account for thousands of jobs in the EU. Because it is precisely these jobs that trade defense instruments are intended to defend, the EU has to reconsider the best use of trade defense instruments in the context of a global economy marked by the growing fragmentation and complexity of the production process and supply chains and the growth of major new economic actors. According to an EC Green Paper,[22] from the perspective of trade defense instruments, the challenge is to consider whether EU rules take sufficient account of the reality of outsourced production by European businesses, which is in competition with EU-based production and might therefore be negatively affected by trade defense measures. It is not in the EU's long-term economic interest to tolerate dumping, even where it benefits European companies that have outsourced production to third-world countries. But

---

[21] European Commission (2007) 'European Commission proposes end to anti-dumping duties on energy saving lightbulbs in one year', EC Press Release, August 29. http://europa.eu/rapid/pressReleasesAction.do?reference=IP/07/1261   (last accessed September 30, 2011).

[22] See footnote 2.

the EU also needs to reflect on the fact that action to limit the injury caused by dumping can have an impact on employment and the viability of EU companies that are operating legitimately through outsourced production. Striking the right balance between free trade and fair trade is crucial.

In this context, the question that arises is: are the European producers which have outsourced part of their activities abroad entitled to challenge the anti-dumping action? According to the standing requirements for the definition of Community industry in both anti-dumping and anti-subsidy cases, both Philips and GE reached the current threshold of 25% of active support. However, companies that import or are related to the exporters should remain excluded from standing assessments. That is why Osram challenged their qualification as community industries. In this connection, the above question amounts to the question of whether special treatment should be given in anti-dumping investigations when a European company located abroad is involved. The EC practice does already allow special treatment for EU companies that conduct partial outsourcing to be considered as part of the EU industry. Such practice is fair and should not be modified. However, EU companies that only (or mostly) import or are related to exporters in third-world countries should remain excluded from the definition of the Community industry (as this is clearly stipulated in Article 4 of the WTO anti-dumping agreement and in Article 4(1a) of the basic EC anti-dumping regulation).

The EC's approach in this case is in line with EC practice: when Osram launched the anti-dumping investigation, the EC seemed to be determined not to tolerate the so-called unfair trade practices. Even when the anti-dumping measures had been imposed, European companies which had invested abroad mobilized various stakeholders (particularly the member states) to demonstrate disapproval at anti-dumping measures, while exploring the possibility to participate and prove they were not dumping goods on the European market, resulting in the EC changing their minds.

(3) *Discussions*

The light bulbs and footwear cases also illustrated another problem in the context of determining what is in the wider economic interest of the EU. In the majority of cases, especially those which do not concern consumer products, the impact of anti-dumping measures on the prices paid by the consumer have typically not been significant. Nonetheless, it is important to reflect on the question of how consumer interests can be better reflected in anti-dumping investigations, and if any measures can be taken to ensure this. The EU is one of the few trade defense users that applies a public interest test in the form of the community interest rule before anti-dumping measures are applied. The community interest rule states that measures can only be imposed when the EC determines that imposing them is not against the wider interest of the EU economy. However, since consumers are not always present in investigations to make their interests known, consumer interests are not adequately taken into consideration, especially when trade defense instruments are applied to finished consumer products. However, fearing that doing this would lead to conflict between the different stakeholders, the EC has thus far been reluctant to be more proactive in soliciting input from consumers' associations.

The EU not only needs to strike a balance between producers, retailers and consumers, but also between trade policy instruments and broader community policy objectives such as climate security, social and environmental standards.

III. How a Trade Dispute Escalates Amid Cross-Use of Trade Defense Instruments and the WTO Dispute Settlement Mechanism

An Overview of China's Trade Defense Instruments

The most controversial part of China's trade policy adjustment efforts in the years after its WTO accession was in the area of trade defense mechanisms. Again, there are two aspects to building a trade defense mechanism: one is reforming and adjusting current trade relief regulations and measures that are inconsistent with WTO requirements, and the other is creating a WTO-compatible trade defense mechanism.

The most important first step was building China's own anti-dumping and countervailing system. China promulgated Regulations on Anti-dumping and Countervailing Duties in 1997. As China repealed import quotas, import licenses, and most other traditional non-tariff barriers as part of its efforts to comply with its commitments upon WTO accession, other ways to protect domestic industries against unfair or improper trade practices were sought. In October 2001, three regulations were introduced that formed the basis of China's new trade remedy system: Regulations on Anti-dumping Duties; Regulations on Countervailing Duties; and Regulations on Safeguard Measures, which were again amended on 31 March 2004 in accordance with the Decision of the State Council on Amending Anti-dumping Regulations.

Introducing WTO-compatible anti-dumping, countervailing, and safeguard measures was the only feasible way to move against unfair trade practices. Anti-dumping was the most-used tool in this regard during the post-WTO era, with cases in the steel and petrochemical industries. Countervailing and safeguard measures are still symbolic at this moment, but they could become important trade remedies in the future, especially safeguard measures that target so-called import surges.

However, to some policy analysts and scholars, these three regulations are not enough to establish a comprehensive trade defense mechanism. They strongly favor adopting other measures to complement the three basic regulations, such as increasing financial subsidies to domestic agriculture. In its accession negotiations, China promised that agricultural support would not surpass 8.5%. However, current agricultural support is much lower than that. So there is room to increase financial support to domestic agriculture while still complying with WTO rules.

An Analysis of China's Anti-dumping Practices

The following provides an analysis of Chinese anti-dumping practices since the country adopted the first Anti-dumping Regulation in 1997.

According to WTO statistics, China investigated 141 cases of dumping between 1997 and June 2008, and implemented 108 anti-dumping measures. As a new member of the WTO, China has become a major user of anti-dumping rules. Before its accession to the WTO, China initiated 33 anti-dumping investigations under the 1997 Regulations.[23] The first anti-dumping investigation was launched in late 1997 on imports of newsprints from Canada, the United States and South Korea.[24]

The number of anti-dumping cases has increased sharply since China's WTO accession. China has initiated 121 investigations since 1 January 2002, while imports have surged dramatically as a result of continuous trade liberalization. Anti-dumping actions have become an important measure to ensure fair competition and to protect the interests of domestic industries. China's anti-dumping investigations are targeted mostly at Japan, South Korea, the United States, Taiwan, the EU, Russia and Singapore.

---

[23] 6 of the 33 cases were terminated without the imposition of anti-dumping duties due to a negative determination on injury.

[24] Yin, J. Z. (2003). China: How to fight the anti-dumping war. *China and the World Economy*, 3.

Since its WTO accession, China's trade has expanded considerably, and the country has become a key export market economy like Japan, South Korea, US, Taiwan and the EU. Surging trade with these economies has also resulted in a growing number of trade disputes. By 30 June 2008, China had initiated 28 anti-dumping cases against Japan, 23 of which were applied on imports from Japan. This is followed by Korea (with 26 cases and 20 measures applied), the US (with 20 cases and 16 measures applied), Taiwan (with 14 cases and 11 measures applied), and the EU (with 8 cases and 6 measures applied).

China's anti-dumping cases are mostly applied on products like industrial chemicals (61.7%), plastics and rubber (18.4%), and wood pulp and paper (6.4%). Other smaller categories include base metals (3.6%), mineral products (2.8%), and textiles (2.8%). Industrial chemicals clearly dominate China's anti-dumping cases, accounting for 87 out of 141 cases initiated since 1997. The sector is also the most frequent subject of anti-dumping cases at an international level. Generally speaking, chemical products involved in anti-dumping investigations are relatively new to China. Because of this, China depends on imports and is therefore an attractive market for foreign producers.

Though the chemical industry is China's third largest after textiles and machinery, China has a trade deficit in the sector. In fact, China is the world's second largest consumer of basic chemical products after the US, and China is heavily dependent on imports of these chemical products. With the commitment to lower tariffs on chemicals after its WTO accession, domestic producers in the sector are facing increasing competition from imports. Consequently, the Chinese government has carried out numerous anti-dumping investigations and, in some cases, imposed measures to protect its chemical producers.

Article 56 of the Anti-dumping Regulation provides: If any country (region) imposes anti-dumping measures on the products exported from the People's Republic of China in a discriminatory manner, China may, on the basis of the actual situations, take corresponding measures against that country (region). It appears that China may use the anti-dumping remedy as a legitimate retaliatory tool to counteract unfair foreign anti-dumping measures against Chinese goods. This explains why China, which is a frequent target of anti-dumping measures in foreign markets, has used anti-dumping rules to retaliate against discriminative anti-dumping measures, although it is not clear what relevance this provision has to the administration of China's anti-dumping remedies. It should be noted that applying the authority that this provision seems to provide could result in WTO inconsistencies.

Case Studies

(1) *Case history*

Case 3 and Case 4: Anti-dumping measures on iron and steel fasteners

On 26 September 2007, the Commission received a complaint from the European Industrial Fasteners Institute (EIFI, the complainant), lodged pursuant to Article 5 of Council Regulation (EC) No. 384/96 on protection against dumped imports from countries not members of the European Community (the basic Regulation), on behalf of producers representing more than 25% of the total Community production of certain iron or steel fasteners.

The EC came to a final decision on 26 January 2009 to impose anti-dumping tariffs on imports of some Chinese steel and iron fasteners, ranging from 26.5% to as high as 85%.

China then retaliated by launching its own anti-dumping investigation into imports of screws and bolts made in the European Union. In the meantime, China requested consultation on 31 July 2009, and later launched a complaint in the WTO on 4 August 2009.[25] China imposed preliminary anti-dumping duties on the fasteners for six months starting on 28 December 2009. On 28 June 2010, China announced that it would impose tariffs on certain EU-made iron and steel fasteners ranging from 6.1% to 26% for five years beginning from the next day. China's imposition of final anti-dumping duties on steel fasteners imported from the European Union is regarded as

---

[25] See WTO DS 397. EC — Definitive Anti-Dumping Measures on Certain Iron or Steel Fasteners from China. On 12 October 2009, China requested the establishment of a panel which the WTO Dispute Settlement Body (DSB) established on 23 October 2009. Brazil, Canada, Chile, Colombia, India, Japan, Norway, Chinese Taipei, Thailand, Turkey and the US reserved their third-party rights. On 30 November 2009, the European Communities requested the Director-General to determine the composition of the panel, which he did on 9 December 2009. On 1 April 2010, the Chairman of the panel informed the DSB that the panel expected to complete its work in September 2010. On 3 December 2010, the panel ruling was circulated to parties. On 10 January 2011, the EU and China requested the DSB to adopt a draft decision extending the 60-day time period stipulated in Article 16.4 of the Dispute Settlement Understanding (DSU) to 25 March 2011. At its meeting on 25 January 2011, the DSB agreed that, upon a request by the European Union and China, the DSB shall, no later than 25 March 2011, adopt the panel report, unless the DSB decides by consensus not to do so or the European Union or China notifies the DSB of its decision to appeal pursuant to Article 16.4 of the DSU.

an 'eye for an eye' measure in response to the loss of trade in nuts and bolts worth hundreds of millions of euros.

On 13 May 2010, the EU filed a complaint against China at the WTO over preliminary anti-dumping duties that China imposed on fasteners for six months starting on 28 December 2009.[26] The EU challenged anti-dumping duties imposed by Beijing on imports of screws, nuts and bolts which accounted for some 140 million euros (179 million US dollars) of the EU exports to China per year, taking issue with the way China calculated the extent of dumping of nuts and bolts and the resulting penalty taxes imposed on imports from the EU.

(2) *Discussions*

It is now safe to argue that China was basically attacking the EU's anti-dumping instrument in an unprecedentedly wholesale way. This explained nothing but its anger towards the EU on the fundamentals of the trade defense instrument and its applications. It also provides an insight into how a trade dispute escalates amid cross-use of trade defense instruments and the WTO dispute settlement mechanism.

IV. Comments in Light of WTO Consistency

Given the availability of various trade defense instruments, both the EU and China are in a position to use each trade defense instrument according to its relevance to a given situation. As a matter of fact, almost all trade defense action by the EU takes the form of anti-dumping measures.

Needless to say, both parties' trade defense instruments and their applications are not impeccable. In this regard, while the EC is understandably responsive to its member governments, it remains untouched amid criticism from its trade partners against its trade defense instruments and its practice. In fact, the EC's stance seems even more stubborn when external evaluations seem to approve the EU's trade defense instruments and its current practice. As illustrated by the iron and steel fasteners case, the EC's role in the use of trade defense instruments results in dissatisfaction from its trade partners that manifests itself in trade disputes.

---

[26] See DS407. China — Provisional Anti-Dumping Duties on Certain Iron and Steel Fasteners from the European Union.

Fortunately, the light bulbs and leather shoes cases served as an internal catalyst and the iron and steel fasteners case as an external catalyst for the EU to overhaul its trade defense instruments, including its anti-dumping mechanism, which was launched in December 2007. This was given an impetus by the ruling of the WTO on the iron and steel fasteners case. The European Commission is scheduled to unveil its plan to reform the EU's trade defense system.

The iron and steel fasteners case suggests that the EU's reform of its anti-dumping remedy shall proceed in order to mend the inconsistency between the trade defense instrument and the EU's obligations within the legal framework of the WTO. Though the panel's ruling of 3 December 2010 was trimming, as WTO panels sometimes seem to be, by upholding some of China's complaints while refuting the others,[27] the ruling turned out to justify China's anger to a certain degree. The panel found that Article 9(5) of the Basic Regulation was inconsistent with Articles 6.10, 9.2 and 18.4 of the Anti-dumping Agreement, Article I(1) of GATT 1994 and Article XVI(4) of the WTO Agreement. This was because, with respect to producers from non-market economy countries, the individual treatment test embodied in this provision conditioned the calculation of individual dumping margins and the imposition of individual duties upon the fulfillment of certain criteria. The panel also found that the application of Article 9(5) of the Basic Regulation in the fasteners investigation was inconsistent with Articles 6.10 and 9.2 of the Anti-dumping Agreement. The panel further found that the EU investigating authorities acted inconsistently with Articles 3.1 and 3.2 of the Anti-dumping Agreement with respect to the consideration of the

---

[27] The panel rejected China's claims with respect to the standing determination, definition of domestic industry, product under consideration, dumping determination, price undercutting determination, treatment of imports from non-sampled producers, consideration of the consequent impact of dumped imports on the domestic industry, non-disclosure of the identity of the complainants and the supporters of the complaint, confidential treatment of the Eurostat data on total EU production of fasteners, procedural aspects of the domestic industry definition, and the amount of time provided for responses to requests for information. The panel found that China's claims concerning the definition of like product, alleged non-disclosure of aspects of the normal value determination, and the procedural aspects of the domestic industry definition were not within its terms of reference and declined to make findings on these claims. Further, it applied judicial economy with respect to some of China's claims regarding the Basic Regulation and the Definitive Regulation.

volume of dumped imports, Articles 3.1 and 3.5 with respect to the causation analysis, Articles 6.4 and 6.2 with respect to aspects of the normal value determination, Article 6.5.1 with respect to non-confidential versions of questionnaire responses of two European producers, and Article 6.5 with respect to confidential treatment of information in the questionnaire response of an Indian producer and confidential treatment of the Eurostat data on the total EU production of fasteners.

The panel recommended that the DSB request the EU to bring its measures into conformity with its obligations under the WTO Agreement. Although the panel declined to make a suggestion on how the DSB recommendations and rulings may be implemented by the EU, the recommendations shed light on how the EU's anti-dumping instrument should be restructured.

In light of the debates among various stakeholders regarding the community interest test, the review was expected to take more into account those EU companies which now produce goods outside the EU for import into the bloc, outsource some steps in the production process, or operate supply chains that stretch beyond the EU market. It is indeed time for the EU to adjust its anti-dumping instrument, which was most frequently used and often controversial, not only to protect its industry in Europe, but also in other regions where European industries are located due to the international division of labor. The obstacles to revising trade defense instruments are difficult to overcome. For example, this requires flexible treatment or even raising the standing requirements. However, for some sectors, especially those that are very fragmented due to the presence of large numbers of active SMEs, or those with only a very small European federation that lacks the resources to facilitate the preparation of a complaint and coordinate joint action, it is already very hard to reach the current threshold of 25% of active support. Increasing this threshold would result in these sectors being dispossessed of their right to defend their legitimate interests against unfairly traded goods.

In this context, it may be appropriate to introduce more flexibility, provided that any adjustment of measures fully reflects the objective findings of the case. Such flexibility would be limited to downward adjustments by the EU's lesser duty rule, which requires that duties be set at the injury margin or the dumping margin, whichever is lower. In theory, it could also extend to the ability to exempt certain products from duties due to community interests. If taken, this move would ease the tension between the EU and China, which is a major production base in the world.

Lastly, it should be borne in mind that the principal concern of the EU's trade defense instruments is responding to the effect of unfair competition. The above cases have raised, among other things, the question of using the community interest test to weigh the impact of measures on the overall coherence of EU policy. For example, the EU might consider whether, in some cases, anti-dumping measures reduce the effectiveness of EU development assistance to a given country.

V. Concluding Remarks

It is noted that there is no real alternative to the use of trade defense instruments in the absence of competition rules that have been agreed upon at an international level. Other trade policies may diminish the number of circumstances that can give rise to unfairly traded goods, but they cannot completely prevent it from happening. Furthermore, there is no other international instrument or rule available, other than the trade defense instrument, that can give relief against unfair trade practices. The use of trade defense instruments has become a prominent part of China-EU trade relations not only because the use of anti-dumping remedies has increased and spread among Chinese exports to such an extent that it now represents a systemic threat to bilateral trade relations, but because the trade defense instruments themselves and their use have exacerbated trade disputes. A crucial issue now lies ahead: downplay trade disputes or remedy trade defense instruments?

Against the backdrop of trade disputes exacerbated by the cross-use of trade defense instruments, should both sides downplay trade disputes or remedy trade defense instruments? On the Chinese side, the government has portrayed trade disputes as 'normal' to maintain harmony in the overall relationship with trade partners, as well as to prepare their own companies for a potential rise in the frequency and severity of disputes. The emphasis on downplaying disputes appears to set a new guideline for Chinese trade officials to moderate their responses to the EU on market access and other issues. This implies that China may be less inclined to retaliate directly in response to the threat of trade actions, and may acquiesce to priority trade demands under intense pressure to avoid the spillover of trade disputes into other areas of the bilateral relationship. There seems to be nothing wrong about the new approach. After all, the tit-for-tat response from the Chinese side has been nothing more than to take WTO-compatible measures in trade disputes rather than to retaliate in kind as it did against South Korean and Japanese safeguard actions in the late 1990s.[28]

However, there is also nothing wrong in the effort to remedy trade defense instruments. The light bulb and leather shoes issues offer only a small glimpse into the complex political economy behind the EU's anti-dumping measures. The use of trade defense instruments is a result of the internal interactions of interested parties within the institutional framework of trade defense instruments. It could also be a tit-for-tat response to the other party's use of the latter's trade defense instrument. Externally, trade disputes are often triggered by the use of trade defense instruments by the other party. Such disputes can escalate due to the cross-use of trade defense instruments.

While China is ambitious in amending the current Anti-dumping Agreement, a minimal approach that focuses on reforms that ensure less contingent protection would be a step in the right direction. It is anticipated that only reforms in anti-dumping measures and returning to international price discrimination as the sole test for unfair behavior can reduce the possibility of trade disputes between China and the EU.

---

[28] For an analysis of China-Korea and China-Japan disputes, see Kong, Q. (2002). Will China behave in the WTO Dispute Settlement Mechanism? In John Wong and Yongnian Zheng (eds), *China's Fourth Generation of Leadership*, World Scientific: Singapore.

CHAPTER 4

THE EU'S MONITORING OF CHINA'S COMPLIANCE WITH WTO OBLIGATIONS

To World Trade Organization (WTO) members, admitting a country with a rapidly expanding economy into the WTO was a great experiment, as the country would have a significant impact on global resource allocation. Many of China's trading partners are worried. Some developing countries fear that global demand for their exports will shrink and that their FDI inflows will fall, given China's potential to pump out a seemingly unlimited supply of labor-intensive exports, and that FDI may bypass them for China's vast market. Some industrial countries worry that China's exports might flood their domestic markets.

To safeguard itself, the EU, like the US, imposed a comprehensive protocol upon China which has more far-reaching obligations beyond the WTO. The EU also kept a close watch on China's behavior in the WTO. With no task force to monitor China's compliance, the EU has taken full advantage of the built-in mechanisms in the WTO, i.e., the Trade Policy Review Mechanism and the Dispute Settlement Mechanism, as well as other measures (including bilateral channels and unilateral measures). After all, China's motivation for joining the WTO is rooted in the realization that it needs an external impetus to overcome domestic obstacles to further reforms and protection of its trade interests.

For the EU, the real question is how to encourage China to, on the one hand, change its economy into one that relies more on domestic demand than on export, and one that, on the other, allows market access to more imports and protects intellectual property rights (IPRs). Therefore, monitoring should be conducted to facilitate smooth and thus healthy China-EU trade relations, which will ultimately hinge on the EU's patience and skills in dealing with a rising China.

I. Introduction

China's accession to the WTO on 11 December 2001 was a historic event. For WTO members, admitting China into the world trading system was a great experiment. Indeed, China is a huge country, with a rapidly expanding economy in which the government plays a significant role in making resource allocation decisions.

It was uncertain at the time of accession whether China's economic system would mesh well with WTO rules and the generally market-oriented economies of its trading partners. Moreover, in the history of the world trading system, never has a country of such trading importance and system incompatibility with WTO norms been admitted.

It was anticipated that given China's weight of global trade, the anticipated gigantic surge in trade would disrupt the markets of its trading partners, and the rule-based multilateral trading system would be endangered if China opted to ignore WTO rules. To preempt such moves, the EU, like the US, had successfully forced China to accept a comprehensive protocol which commits China to more far-reaching obligations beyond the WTO.

Although the EU did not follow the US in forming a task force to monitor China's compliance with WTO commitments, it has taken full advantage of the built-in mechanisms of the WTO, i.e., the Trade Policy Review Mechanism (TPRM) and the Dispute Settlement Mechanism (DSM), as well as employed other measures (including bilateral channels and unilateral measures) to this end.

It should be pointed out that the EU's monitoring of China's WTO compliance has two implications for trade disputes. On one hand, the monitoring will help locate China's compliance shortfalls and help China to rectify these shortfalls, thus mitigating the possibility of trade disputes. On the other, if not properly carried out, monitoring will make existing problems more complicated and may even trigger new disputes, particularly given that the monitoring mechanism is deployed with special vigilance when it comes to China.

II. Focal Points of China's WTO Compliance

China has made some progress in formally meeting its WTO accession commitments, but there are still complaints about market access, inadequate protection of intellectual property rights, and a lack of transparency coupled with the arbitrariness of Chinese procedures in anti-dumping investigations against EU exports to China. Failures to comply persist in a number of areas of key importance to the EU. While China has generally reduced tariffs in accordance with its accession commitments, it still maintains non-tariff barriers and is erecting new non-tariff barriers that harm European interests by effectively limiting market access for European goods and services. China continues to tolerate rampant piracy of copyrighted European material, which costs European industries billions in lost profits each year.

Market Access

Indeed, the commitments made by China in the context of its WTO accession secured improved access of EU firms to China's market. Many import tariffs and other non-tariff barriers were sharply and permanently lifted. While China has made good progress in implementing its WTO commitments, there are still outstanding problems. China has just lost the case on Measures Affecting Imports of Automobile Parts in the WTO, and that is not all. Disagreements over Chinese tax and tariff discrimination against other products imported from the EU and market access are also at the forefront of the trade agenda.

European services companies are having difficulties breaking into the Chinese market as they often face discrimination. Since 2001, although China has signed agreements to open its market, only 7 out of 22,000 telecoms licenses have been granted to foreign companies. China maintains investment and ownership caps in many strategic sectors such as banking, construction and telecommunications. Foreign law firms in China are not allowed to employ Chinese lawyers and are not permitted to participate in bar exams to gain Chinese qualifications.

Lax Intellectual Property Rights Enforcement

Infringement of European IPR is often cited as an unfair trade practice on the part of the Chinese. For European firms in China, IPR theft remains a huge problem. More than 80% of all counterfeit goods seized at European borders in 2006 came from China. Seven in ten European firms operating in China say that they have been victims of IPR violations. In 2007, European manufacturers estimated that IPR theft cost them 20% of their potential revenues in China.

Correspondingly, Chinese companies are subjected to more IPR infringement investigations. Chinese goods displayed in trade fairs in Europe are often found to be unauthorized copies of European products and are thus confiscated by European customs authorities. In some cases, the responsible persons in these Chinese companies were prosecuted for IPR infringement.[1]

Though China might cite its continuous efforts at revamping its laws and redoubling its efforts at enforcement, the incidence of copyright piracy in particular is not reported to be declining. A perceived failure to do much to address the problem successfully is one of the reasons why some Europeans have been advocating tough measures against China.

On an average basis, IPR infringement in China is not much worse than anywhere else. But since China is the world's largest and fastest growing economy, the problem is put under the spotlight and thus magnified. Indeed, the Chinese government has taken several steps to protect IPR and is feeling at a loss as to what more it can do. However, from a purely legalistic point of view, the government can do more by getting rid of the minimum thresholds for prosecution, destroying confiscated materials rather than removing their labels and reintroducing these products into the supply chain, and granting copyright protection for products awaiting approval for distribution in China.

Anti-dumping Procedures

In the area of anti-dumping, China's increasing resort to trade defense instruments may likewise lead to dissatisfaction among EU exporters to China. Since its WTO accession, China has become one of the most frequent users of the anti-dumping mechanism among WTO members. The EU, together with other WTO members, has also raised the issue of the arbitrary imposition of anti-dumping investigations and called for transparency in investigation procedures.[2] This accumulating dissatisfaction may also lead to trade disputes between China and the EU.

---

[1] For example, at the March 2008 CeBit technology trade fair — Europe's largest gadget confab — in Hannover, Germany, police raided 51 exhibitors' booths for suspected patent violations, among which 24 were from China. See http://news.cnet.com/8301-10784_3-9887955-7.html (last accessed September 30, 2011).

[2] See, for example, the EC Communications to the Trade Policy Review Body concerning China's trade policy review (WT/TPR/M/161).

Industrial Policies

China's longstanding sector-specific industrial policies have an impact on the competitiveness of EU firms in China and may serve as *de facto* barriers to market access for EU firms. In 17 September 2003, the EU successfully committed China to a dialogue to cope with issues regarding industrial policies.[3] In spite of this, the issue repeatedly comes to the forefront of China-EU trade relations. For example, during Trade Policy Reviews, the EC raised the issues twice, accusing China of failing to comply with WTO rules that directly or indirectly impact competitiveness and productivity. In fact, in the semiconductor chips case raised in the WTO, it was these industrial policies that triggered complaints from the EU as well as the US.[4] Also, in the auto parts dispute raised in the WTO,[5] the EC again attacked China's automobile industrial policy, i.e., the Policy on the Development of Automotive Industry.[6]

China's Raw Material Export

In January 2004, China sharply restricted its coke exports, claiming increasing internal demand and production cutbacks due to environmental reasons. Following several rounds of threats and ensuing consultations in both 2004 and 2005, China returned to the old system, which resulted in a return to traditional export volumes and reasonable price levels. China is committed to reforming its export licensing systems to make it conform better to WTO rules.[7]

---

[3] Minutes of the Meeting for Establishing the Framework of the Industrial Policy Dialogue, available at http://ec.europa.eu/enterprise/enterprise_policy/gov_relations/china_regul_coop_dialogue/minutes_17-09-2003.pdf (last accessed June 30, 2008).

[4] In order to encourage foreign chips manufacturers to build facilities in China, China places a 17% tax on semiconductors but gives local manufacturers rebates, thereby providing the latter with a substantial advantage. On 17 March, the EU and the US lodged complaints concerning the chips tax rebate. The dispute ended with China phasing out its tax rebate policy in July 2004.

[5] China — Measures Affecting Imports of Automobile Parts, see WTO DS339, available at http://www.wto.org/english/tratop_e/dispu_e/cases_e/ds339_e.htm (last accessed September 30, 2011).

[6] Order No. 8 of the National Development and Reform Commission, 21 May 2004.

[7] The EU launched an anti-dumping investigation into China's coke and has imposed a relative tariff of 32.6 euros per ton since 2000. After the EC's suspension

Several Chinese companies extract and process rare earths and therefore have a strong interest in protecting their processing branches. The EC pointed the Chinese government to the fact that the EU industry cannot obtain the required quantities of export licences. China decided, with EU intervention, to abolish its VAT reimbursement system on copper that was not viewed as WTO-compatible. However, trade in non-ferrous metals is still subject to export taxes and other trade obstacles.

Exchange Rate Policy

The exchange rate policy of a WTO member is by nature not regulated by the WTO. However, there have been complaints that China intervenes massively in the foreign exchange market to maintain a hugely undervalued renminbi. This has helped to boost its international competitive position by pursuing the currency peg in 2005 or the 'managed floating exchange rate based on market supply and demand' thereafter as a result of the exchange rate system reform. Accordingly, China's exchange rate policy has gained a hold in trade policy debates.

There has been a growing chorus calling for the value of the renminbi to be raised or immediately floated to let market forces decide its value. In the eyes of critics, the core of the matter is that China's exchange rate policy allows Chinese firms to export goods to the EU at artificially low prices, resulting in job losses in the EU. However, Chinese processing industries are unhappy to see a sharp rise of the renminbi's value, which would eat out a substantial part of their thin profits from the export market. Moreover, there is some justification for China's fears that an abrupt move to a freely floating exchange rate now, particularly if accompanied by abolition of their controls on financial outflows, could trigger capital flight and jeopardize their economy in view of the fragility of their banking system.

---

of the anti-dumping duty, the Chinese government adopted an export license system and a quota administration system for coke export on 1 January 2004. On 31 March 2004, the EC responded by threatening to refer the dispute to the WTO dispute settlement mechanism. On 9 May 2004, the EC further threatened that failure to reach an agreement on coke exports within five days would lead to the initiation of the first complaint against China in the WTO. China angrily responded with an immediate withdrawal of tax rebates for coke exports on 24 May. On 26 May 2004, the EC issued an ultimatum prompting China to cancel coke export restrictions by 28 May to avoid an imminent dispute in the WTO. The two parties reached a settlement on 28 May.

Accordingly, mounting pressure from the EU as well as the US has induced only slight changes in the Chinese exchange rate regime. The renminbi has appreciated about 20% in value against the dollar since July 2005. However, to the dismay of the EU, the renminbi has weakened some 10% against the euro during this same period, which is damaging to European competitiveness. Economists argued that the problem is with the weak dollar and not the strong renminbi. So long as the Chinese currency continues to track the dollar, nothing can be done about this.

Critics contend that the undervalued renminbi violates Article XV(4) of the General Agreement on Tariffs and Trade (GATT) and the WTO Agreement on Subsidies and Countervailing Measures. The governments of China's trade partners are considering bringing a formal complaint to the WTO — to treat China's alleged currency manipulation as a source of dumping or countervailable subsidies that would permit the imposition of antidumping or countervailing duties on Chinese imports.[8] Similarly, while a policy case against the renminbi value can be made in the International Monetary Fund (IMF), a legal case has no supporting precedent and faces an uphill battle.[9]

III. Methods of Monitoring

Multilateral Means

To monitor China's compliance with WTO obligations, the EU employs multilateral means, such as the WTO's Dispute Settlement Mechanism (DSM) and Trade Policy Review Mechanism (TPRM), that are built within the WTO framework.

The DSM is the central pillar of the multilateral trading system, and the WTO's unique contribution to the stability of the global economy. Without a means to settle disputes, the rule-based system would be less

---

[8] For a detailed comparison of China's exchange rate policy and the WTO agreements, see Hufbauer, G. C., Y. Wong, and K. Sheth (2006). *US-China Trade Disputes: Rising Tide, Rising Stakes.* The Peterson Institute for International Economics, August, pp. 17–24.

[9] Under IMF rules, China has the right to peg its currency, but not to intervene massively in the foreign exchange market. For a systematic analysis of the compatibility of China's exchange rate policy and the articles of the IMF, see *Ibid.* pp. 24–26.

effective because the rules would be impossible to enforce. The mechanism underscores the rule of law, and makes the trading system more secure and predictable. The mechanism is based on clearly defined rules, with timetables for completing a case. First rulings made by a panel — unless these are appealed against — are endorsed automatically by the Dispute Settlement Body comprising the WTO's full members.

A dispute arises when a country adopts a trade policy measure or acts in such a way that one or more fellow WTO members consider such actions to be violations of WTO agreements, or fails to abide by its obligations. The EU has not hesitated to take advantage of the WTO dispute settlement mechanism when China is perceived to have failed to abide by its obligations. Since China's WTO accession, the EC has launched five complaints against China.[10] The latest case took place on 25 July 2011 when the EU formally requested consultation concerning China's definitive anti-dumping duties on X-Ray security inspection equipment from the EU.[11]

However, the aim of such consultations is not to pass judgement but to settle disputes, through consultations if possible. By July 2008, only two of the nearly eight cases against China had reached the full panel process. The rest have either been classified as settled 'out of court' or remain in a prolonged consultation phase. Consultation reduces the possibility of confrontation.

The EU also uses the regular TPRM of the WTO to address its concerns. Trade Policy Reviews (TPR) are mandated in the WTO agreements with the purpose of regularly examining and evaluating members' trade-related policies. Significant developments that may have an impact on the global trading system are also monitored. The EU, which treats China as an important trading partner, uses the review to press China on key issues such as government interference, transparency, standards, IPR protection and

---

[10] See WTO Secretariat, Disputes by country/territory, http://www.wto.org/english/tratop_e/dispu_e/dispu_by_country_e.htm (last accessed November 30, 2011).

[11] The European Union claims that the measure is inconsistent with various provisions of the Anti-Dumping Agreement related to the process of the anti-dumping investigation (including failure to provide access to relevant information and insufficient explanation of the basis for the determinations), as well as the anti-dumping determination at issue (absence of objective examination of the effect of the dumped imports on prices in the domestic market and absence of objective determination of causality).

discrimination against EU firms.[12] China has undergone five rounds of transitional TPR[13] and two rounds of regular TPR at the WTO, and passed both reviews.

However, according to some observers, China has frustrated the effectiveness of the WTO's Transitional Review Mechanism (TRM), thereby preventing it from becoming a robust mechanism for assessing China's compliance and for placing multilateral pressure on China to address shortfalls. The TRM is a central element of China's WTO accession arrangement, and its failure to perform as intended is a serious policy concern that demands attention. China has taken deliberate actions to make the TRM process meaningless and must therefore ultimately bear the blame for the TRM's failure. However, the US and other WTO members are also at fault for allowing the marginalization of the TRM.[14]

Bilateral Means

At the bilateral level, there are ministerial meetings, meetings between senior officials, an annual Joint Committee at ministerial level and an Economic and Trade Working Group. At the 2007 EU-China Summit, a High Level Economic and Trade Dialogue mechanism (HLM) was established, as well as High Level Dialogues on exchange rate issues and on macroeconomic issues.[15] The HLM, which institutionalized the dialogue between the EC and the State Council of China at Vice-Premier level, is designed to deal with issues of strategic importance to EU-China trade

---

[12] For example, during the second TPR from 21–23 May 2008, the EU submitted more than 170 questions to China.

[13] The Protocol on the Accession of China designed a Transitional Trade Policy Review specifically for China, which is conducted annually for eight consecutive years starting 2001.

[14] US-China Economic and Security Review Commission (2004). *China in the World Trade Organization: Compliance, Monitoring, and Enforcement.* http://www.uscc.gov/annual_report/2004/04reportpage7.pdf (last accessed September 30, 2011).

[15] The HLM was agreed upon at the November 2007 Summit by President Barroso and Premier Wen Jiabao, to address the imbalance in trade flows between the EU and China. The broad remit of the HLM is to examine the global trading system, strategic bilateral trade-related issues, investment, innovation, technology and IPR, and EU-China economic cooperation. The HLM functions as a complement and reinforcement to established EU-China dialogues.

relations, investment and economic cooperation. At present, there are ongoing negotiations for a Partnership and Cooperation Agreement.[16]

There have also been cooperative efforts on the EU side to encourage China to comply with WTO rules. A typical example of technical assistance is the EC's EU-China Programme to Support China's Integration into the World Trading System. The program is designed, *inter alia*, to assist the Chinese government in implementing its obligations to the WTO as well as to increase the capacity of China in the process of wider economic, regulatory, legal and administrative reform necessary for further trade liberalization in order to promote economic development.

The less visible but flourishing area of exchanges on sectoral policies and technical issues are 'sectoral dialogues' between China and Europe. These dialogues have grown considerably in recent years, covering a wide range of areas from science and technology to enterprise regulation, and from environmental issues to education and the information society. All these bilateral channels can be used to address the EU's concerns related to China's compliance with WTO commitments.

Unilateral Means

Besides multilateral and bilateral means, the EU also employs unilateral means to monitor China's WTO compliance. It has adopted various regulations and directives to compel China to comply with WTO commitments. A typical example is the EU's adoption of product-specific safeguard measures against Chinese textiles and apparel.

Broadly speaking, technical assistance that is designed to help China comply with its WTO obligations belongs to the category of unilateral monitoring means. Immediately after China's accession to the WTO, the EU offered technical expertise in the form of the EU-China Programme for China's Accession to the WTO in order to help China adjust to WTO rules and standards. After this first program, the EU and China embarked on a much more ambitious EU-China Project for Support to China's Integration into the World Trading System, commonly referred to as the EU-China Trade Project (EUTCP). The five-year project started in June 2004, with a pledge of €15 million by Brussel and another €5.6 million by China.

---

[16] http://ec.europa.eu/external_relations/china/dialogue_en.htm (last accessed June 30, 2008).

IV. The EU's and the US's Approach to Monitoring China's Compliance with WTO Commitments

To some extent, both the EU and the US share similar concerns in their trade relations with China. Over the past decade, the widening US-China trade deficit has been a focal point of bilateral relations, and has often been portrayed as a cause for overall US current account imbalances. However, real public concerns are rooted in the perceived economic threat of import competition from China, as well as in areas concerning illegal export subsides, lax enforcement of intellectual property rights, restricted market access, and an undervalued national currency.[17]

These concerns have fueled calls for legislation to prevent unfair trade practices. In February 2005, the US Senate passed the Byrd Amendment, encouraging American companies to file anti-dumping investigation applications by awarding the revenue collected from the resultant tariffs to litigating companies. Other China-specific legislations proposed since then include a bill declaring exchange rate protection to be an illegal subsidy for which US firms can seek compensation.[18]

However, compared with the EU's approach, the US approach towards the monitoring of China's compliance is even more judgmental. Firstly, the EU has been seen to adopt a distinct attitude towards China's rise. The US sees China as a competitor, and is somewhat intolerant of China's rise. Indeed, for the US, its dislike of a strong, prosperous China under an authoritarian state is more palpable than for the EU. The EU and China have pledged to maintain a comprehensive strategic partnership, while the US views China as a stakeholder at best. The political tolerance displayed by the EU, cemented in the 'Comprehensive Strategic Partnership',[19] is supposed to lower the profile of the EU's monitoring.

Moreover, the EU differs from the US on the perception of China's compliance itself, at least during the transitional period. Both the EU and China have recognized that China has achieved a lot since accession, though issues of concern remain. The EU seemed to be sympathetic to the

---

[17] Hufbauer *et al.* (2006). pp. 4–10.

[18] *Ibid.*, p. 23.

[19] In a Joint Statement of the 9th EU-China Summit on 9 September 2006, both parties proclaimed the existence of a comprehensive strategic partnership. Since January 2007, China and EU started negotiating for a comprehensive Partnership and Cooperation Agreement.

immensity of the task with which China is faced, and was found during the transitional period to be more tolerant of cases of non-compliance on the part of China. The EU was more willing to seek solutions through consultations, dialogues and cooperation programmes than the US.[20]

For example, for the first time in the history of the world trading system, a monitoring task force was established by the US under the auspices of the Department of Commerce to monitor Chinese compliance with WTO commitments. As legislative bodies — whether European or American — tend to be more responsive to domestic industrial pressure, the US Trade Representative's Office annually submits a report on China's WTO compliance to the Congress to launch new defense initiatives against China; the EU has not followed this course.

Thirdly, although the EU is a single customs union with a single trade policy and tariff, it takes time to build up consensus among its 27 members. It is difficult for the EU to come to a single policy with regard to China — each member state has its own history of dealing with China, and some of them have competing economic interests. The EU is thus not as efficient as the US in dealing with China.

V. Effects of Monitoring

Positive Effects

On the positive side, monitoring helps China implement its commitments and bring about institutional changes that are necessary for the development of its market economy.

As far as the multilateral mechanisms that are used to monitor China's WTO compliance are concerned, they have the effect of minimizing the occurrence of trade disputes, and keeping these disputes at a manageable level. For example, throughout the years since its accession to the WTO, China has been learning not to view the use of the WTO dispute settlement mechanism as hostile, and instead, to view lengthy negotiations as a normal method that mature trading partners use to resolve their differences. China has also been learning to use the DSM, particularly by way of third-party involvement in disputes, and has become comfortable in using the mechanism.

---

[20] See footnote 1.

Empirical evidence shows that the use of a sound dispute settlement mechanism by one party has the effect of defusing mounting political pressure and the desire to resort to unilateral trade measures on the part of the other party.[21] Disputes between China and the EU cannot be avoided as the volume of trade surges. Fortunately, in this regard, due to the availability of the multilateral monitoring means, i.e., the DSM as well as the TPRM of the WTO, trade disputes between China and the EU are manageable.

Bilateral monitoring means generally generate positive results. The HLM mechanism, for example, provides a new tool to address issues of mutual concern, especially in the areas of investment, market access, IPR protection and other strategic issues related to trade.[22] It can become the perfect venue for resolving some of the disputed issues in the WTO. The consultation phase of the dispute settlement process will be fully utilized and thus ease the stress of a trade dispute.

Negative Effects

However, the scrupulous monitoring of China's WTO compliance has a negative effect. Given that China is a proud nation, excessive use of the trade dispute settlement mechanism and the relentless use of the unilateral monitoring (except technical assistance) means, in particular, can complicate trade issues to become a source of prospective trade disputes between China and the EU. China still prefers a less confrontational approach. It is not difficult to find that China was provoked or felt provoked when its trade partners adopted trade legislation against it or brought it to the WTO Dispute Settlement Body while trade disputes in question were being discussed.

---

[21] It is not difficult to find two disputing countries ceasing their wars of rhetoric after they refer a dispute to an international adjudicatory institutions such as the International Court of Justice or the WTO Dispute Settlement Body. The recent case between Singapore and Malaysia over Pedra Branca is one such example.

[22] From the EU, the meeting was attended by Commissioners Meglena Kuneva (Consumer Protection), Vladimír Špidla (Social Affairs), Janez Potočnik (Research), Andris Piebalgs (Energy), László Kovács (Taxation and Customs), Louis Michel (Development), Stavros Dimas (Environment) and Peter Mandelson (Trade). The group of Commissioners was led by European Commission President Jose Manuel Barroso. It was the largest joint mission abroad for the European Commission in its 50 years of existence.

VI. Monitoring Continues

Not long after China's accession, the EU seemed to have accepted the fact that problems are to some extent unavoidable, given the formidable task which China is faced with; it was therefore more tolerant of non-compliance matters during the transitional period. The EU was willing to seek solutions through consultations, dialogues and cooperation programmes.[23]

Almost all of the specific commitments that China made when it acceded to the WTO were due to be implemented by the end of 2006. While monitoring China's WTO compliance during this period was pursued with leniency, monitoring since 2007 has been enhanced. Accordingly, the EU has been working to hold China fully accountable — just as others hold the EU accountable — as a mature member of the world trading system, placing a strong emphasis on China's adherence to WTO rules.

The monitoring of China's WTO compliance could well be a major EU priority in the coming years to ensure that EU firms benefit fully. From late 2006, the EU intensified its frank bilateral engagement with China. In a late 2007 internal document, the EC Trade Commissioner Mandelson conceded that conciliatory tactics toward Beijing had failed to secure concessions for Europe. He proposed aligning policies more closely with that of the US and called for greater use of trade laws to hit back at Beijing.[24] It also took enforcement actions at the WTO in key areas where dialogues and rules-based DSM had not resolved its WTO-related concerns. For China, it is alarming if this has become the EU's established approach toward its trade relations with China and the monitoring of China's WTO compliance.

---

[23] See footnote 1.

[24] Castle, S. (2007). 'EU-China trade tensions start to heat up', *International Herald Tribune*, November 6.

CHAPTER 5

THE EU'S TRADE POLICY-MAKING MECHANISM

I. Introduction

As the EU plays a larger and more assertive role in the world economy, its trade and investment policies increasingly have the potential to help or hinder Chinese economic interests. As such, disputes may arise where EU trade policies cast a shadow on the efforts of Chinese companies to pursue their interest in the European as well as in the global market. For this reason, it is important for policy makers and traders to understand how and why EU trade policies are crafted in order to represent and defend Chinese interests to the greatest extent possible.

An overview of the EU's trade policy-making mechanism must be made in the context of the institutional development of this treaty-based international organization. Impetus for the formation of the EU came in the aftermath of the devastation of World War II, with the signing of several treaties by six countries — Belgium, France, Germany, Italy, Luxembourg, and the Netherlands. By agreeing to integrate their economies in matters of coal and steel production, trade, and nuclear energy, Europe's leaders hoped to achieve a closer union among the peoples of Europe and avoid another war on the continent.

As a result of the 1957 'Rome Treaties', the European Economic Community (EEC) came into force in January 1958. As a result of political cooperation and economic integration, the Rome Treaty was integrated into the 1991 Maastricht Treaty on European Union (TEU) and the 1997 Treaty of Amsterdam, thus making the EU a treaty-based institutional framework that defines and manages economic and political cooperation among its members.

The legal basis for the EU's trade policy can be dated back to Article 113 of the Rome Treaty. It is not difficult to find that despite substantial changes in the international economic environment and the global trade agenda over the past four decades, Article 113 has been modified only slightly on three occasions. The 1991 TEU deleted and added some text that did not modify the substance of the article. The 1997 Treaty of Amsterdam amended Article 113 (and renumbered it 133) by extending the scope of the common commercial policy from goods to negotiations on services and intellectual property in cases where the Council of Ministers agrees unanimously.[1] The 2000 Treaty of Nice, which is to ratified by each of the EU members, made further changes in the framework for the adoption of agreements in the areas of services and intellectual property.[2] On the other hand, the institutional framework for the formation of commercial policy has evolved over time, as the scope of what constitutes trade policy has increased to incorporate domestic regulations and non-tariff issues.

The thrust behind Article 113 of the Treaty of Rome is to provide for the free movement of goods.[3] The EEC recognized that it required a common external trade policy to prevent one member state from importing foreign goods at cheaper prices due to lower tariffs and then re-exporting the items to another member state with higher tariffs. Article 113 provides the legal framework for trade policy making. Embedded in this provision are two grants of authority for the formation of trade policy: (1) from the member states and their parliaments to the assembly of European states, acting collectively through the Council of Ministers; and (2) from the Council of Ministers to the European Commission.[4]

---

[1] In a 1994 decision, the European Court of Justice had ruled that services and intellectual property are policy areas subject to mixed national and community competence. In such areas, the principle of unanimity is required before any concluded agreement can be adopted. See Young, A. R. (2000). The adaptation of European foreign economic policy: From Rome to Seattle. *Journal of Common Market Studies*, 38(1), pp. 100–101.

[2] Under Nice, agreements in the area of trade in services and commercial aspects of intellectual property can be concluded by qualified majority vote, except when the external negotiation would require the adoption of internal rules, such as taxation, that still requires unanimity. France successfully negotiated a provision requiring cultural issues to be subject to the unanimity principle.

[3] The EEC was designed to merge separate national markets into a single common market that provides free movement of goods, people, capital, and services across borders.

[4] Meunier, S. and K. Nicolaidis (1999). Who speaks for Europe? The delegation of trade authority in the EU. *Journal of Common Market Studies*, 37(3), p. 480.

Article 113 states as follows:

> The common commercial policy shall be based upon uniform principles, particularly in regard to tariff rates, the conclusion of tariff and other agreements, the achievement of uniformity in measures of liberalization, export policy, and measures to protect such as those to be taken in the event of dumping or subsidies.
> The Commission shall submit proposals to the Council for implementing the common commercial policy.
> Where agreements with third countries need to be negotiated, the Commission shall make recommendations to the Council, which shall authorize the Commission to open negotiations.
> The Commission shall conduct these negotiations in consultation with a special committee appointed by the Council to assist the Commission in this task and within the framework of such directives as the Council may issue for it.

II. Agencies Involved in the EU's Trade Policy Making and their Respective Roles

The European Commission

The European Commission is the EU's version of a central executive body, vested with power to propose legislation and common policies. The Commission also acts as the guardian of EU treaties to ensure that EU legislation is implemented by all members.

On the issue of trade, the Commission has broad authority and responsibilities. Most importantly, the Commission develops proposals for the initiation and content of international trade negotiations and negotiates on behalf of the EU. In drawing up trade proposals, the Commission seeks to balance different national and sectoral interests.

Depending on the negotiation and the mandate provided by the Council, the Commission has considerable flexibility in deciding on negotiation tactics. The Commission also has much autonomy in the administration of the EU's trade remedy procedures (anti-dumping, countervailing duties and safeguard procedures) against foreign non-members.

The Commission is headed by twenty commissioners who are nominated by the member states and then selected by consensus for a five-year term. Each commissioner is charged with acting in support of EU needs and goals, independent of instructions from national governments. Most commissioners have held high office in their home countries prior to their duties in Brussels. Each commissioner has an assigned portfolio and can draw on the Commission's administrative staff of 21,000 civil servants (often referred to as Eurocrats) for support. In addition, they are assisted by a small cabinet or team of aides.

As a body, they meet once a week to adopt proposals and finalize Commission policy. When necessary, decisions of the Commission are made by majority vote.

The group of Commission officials directly responsible for trade policy matters is located in the Trade Directorate. The Directorates for the Internal Market and Industrial Affairs, Competition, and Agriculture also have considerable influence in matters of trade policy. Each directorate is headed by a director-general, who is equivalent in rank to the top civil servant in a government ministry. The directors-general report to one of the twenty Commissioners.[5]

The Council of Ministers

While the Commission has the power and responsibility to initiate trade proposals, the Council of Ministers (formally named the Council of the European Union since the Maastricht Treaty went into effect in 1993) has the power to establish objectives for trade negotiations (a negotiating mandate) and the ultimate authority to implement results. As provided for in Article 113, the Commission conducts trade negotiations "within the framework of such directives as the Council may issue to it". As indicated over the years, the Council has very broad powers in the conduct of all bilateral, regional, and multilateral trade negotiations through its role as the main legislative body of the EU.

The Council is composed of ministers from each member government. The ministers represent the interests of their member states. Different ministers participate in the Council depending on the subject matter under discussion. From the mid-1980s, discussions on trade policy have often been on the agenda of the Council of Foreign Ministers although trade

---

[5] Hayes, J.P. (1993). *Making Trade Policy in the European Community*, St. Martin's Press: New York, pp. 33–35.

ministers have occupied the national chairs during discussions of numerous trade matters.[6]

The Treaty of Rome provides that the Council shall make its trade policy decisions by a qualified majority vote (QMV) where formal decisions are required, or by unanimity in some cases affecting trade in services and intellectual property protection. Each member state has a given number of votes determined by a weighting system that takes population and other factors into account. Currently, five member states and twenty-six votes are necessary to form a blocking minority. In practice, however, the Council tends not to vote on major trade issues, but reaches decisions by consensus.

The "133 Committee"

The third institution referred to in the Rome Treaty is a special committee. In light of Article 113, it seems clear that the Council viewed the special committee as its representative or watchdog over the Commission in its work on trade issues. Initially called the 113 Committee but renamed the 133 Committee, it plays a key role in helping member states influence EU trade policy.[7] While the role of the "133 Committee" is formally consultative, the assistance it provides the Commission is at the heart of EU decision making on trade.[8]

The "133 Committee" meets at both the full committee or senior level and at the level of deputies. Charged with overall responsibility for trade policy, the full members (often referred to as *Titulairies*) meet on a monthly basis (except August). Full members tend to be senior civil servants drawn from national ministries of trade, foreign affairs, or finance. Usually enjoying close

---

[6] Composed of the Presidents or Prime Ministers of each member state and the President of the Commission, the Council is the *de facto* top level decision-making body and it meets at least twice a year. Trade issues, however, are generally discussed and settled at levels below the European Council.

[7] The "133 Committee" is also referred to as the "113 Committee" in a number of journals and articles. With the entry into force of the Amsterdam Treaty in 1997, the "113 Committee" was renamed the "133 Committee" as a result of the renumbering of Article 113 of the Treaty of Rome.

[8] Murphy, A. (2000). In the maelstrom of change — Article 113 committee in the governance of external economic policy. In Thomas Christiansen and Emil Kirchner (eds), *Administering the New Europe: Committee Governance in the European Union* MUP: Manchester.

personal relationships with the ministers they serve, they tend to have a good sense of what actions are politically acceptable within their member states. As many full members serve for extended periods of time, they have a reputation for dealing with sensitive issues on an informal basis.

Usually, the "133 Committee" also meets weekly at the level of deputies. The deputies are drawn from member states' permanent delegations based in Brussels. This group focuses more on technical than political issues.

Since the "133 Committee" is an advisory body, no formal votes are recorded and its deliberations are not published. Matters tend to be discussed until a clear consensus or effective majority has been reached, and the commission tends to follow its advice.

According to one interpretation, "the Commission rarely insists on going against the wishes of the Committee (which it is legally entitled to do) for the simple reason that its members reflect the wishes of ministers who ultimately have the power to refuse to conclude the agreement negotiated by the Commission".[9]

Matters which the "133 Committee" wants to refer to the Council tend to be prepared by the Committee of Permanent Representatives (COREPER). Comprising member state officials who are national ambassadors to the EU, their deputies, and a secretariat with a 2,000-strong staff, COREPER is a key group that assists the Council.

The European Parliament

The 626-member European Parliament (EP) plays a limited and mostly indirect role in trade policy, since it cannot enact laws like most parliaments. While the EP can veto legislation in areas such as social policy, agriculture, and the EU's internal market, it does not have a veto power over trade legislation. However, the Lisbon Treaty suggests more room for the EP to play in the field of trade policy.[10] The EP has tried to exert greater

---

[9] Hayes-Renshaw, F. and H. Wallace (1997). *The Council of Ministers*, St. Martin's Press: New York, p. 88.

[10] The Lisbon Treaty, which came into effect on 1 December 2009, massively expands the Parliament's powers in important policy areas such as external trade, monetary policy, energy, agriculture and fisheries, personal data protection, intellectual property rights, public health, and immigration. For an analysis of the EP's power in trade area, see Hillman, J. and D. Kleimann (2010). Trading places: The new dynamics of EU trade policy under the treaty of Lisbon, Economic Policy Paper Series.

influence over trade issues, particularly those that have a heavy regulatory component.

By holding hearings and issuing reports, the EP can influence the atmosphere during the consideration of trade issues. The EP has a history of passing highly critical resolutions on China, usually focusing on Tibet and human rights and Taiwan. Although it rarely debates the broader aspects of the relationship, the EP is an important player, because the EU-China Partnership and Cooperation Agreement (PCA), currently under negotiation, requires its approval. Perhaps reflecting an effort to enhance its powers vis-à-vis the Commission and member states, the EP has in recent years been the driving force behind a number of controversial trade issues that have divided China and Europe. In this regard, the EP Resolution of 5 February 2009 is worth examining. It lists the concerns of the EU, such as counterfeit and pirated goods, product safety, state-led industries, non-tariff barriers and environmental degradation in China.[11] China expressed its unhappiness

---

[11] The EP proposes the following policies, primarily concerned with European trade with China:

- A continuation of the policy of engagement and dialogue and trade-related technical assistance.
- Unprecedented cooperation in order to resolve the current financial and economic crisis, considering it a great opportunity for China and the EU together to show a sense of responsibility and to play their part in helping to resolve this crisis.
- The development of a genuine, fruitful and effective political dialogue: human rights should be an essential and integral part of the relationship and the Human Rights Clause in the PCA should be strengthened. No resorting to protectionism.
- A welcome to investments by China's sovereign wealth funds and state-owned enterprises in the EU, but with transparency in China's financial markets, and at least a code of conduct to ensure the transparency of China's investment operations in the EU market.
- The removal of restrictions on foreign firms in other sectors, especially on cross-border mergers and acquisitions.
- The promotion of full market access in China for EU companies, and the elimination of protectionist practices, excessive bureaucracy, the undervaluing of the renminbi, various subsidies, and the lack of a proper and agreed level of enforcement of intellectual property rights (IPRs).
- China further opening its markets for goods and services and continuing with economic reforms in order to establish a stable, predictable and transparent legal framework for EU companies, especially for small and medium sized enterprises (SMEs).

about the criticisms made and its 'intrusion' into what are regarded as domestic issues. China is particularly unhappy with the EP's stress "that the new EU-China PCA should aim to establish free and fair trade based on the enforcement of clauses on human rights, environmental, sustainable development and social issues". A Free Trade Agreement is not being negotiated,

- The removal from the draft Chinese Postal Law of a provision that would hamper foreign express services.
- The adoption of international standards for products and services in China, welcoming the increased Chinese participation in international standard-setting bodies, which should be reciprocated by EU participation in China's own standard-setting bodies.
- The abolition of trade-distorting export restrictions such as Chinese export taxes on raw materials. (Parliament underlines that it will evaluate all future trade agreements with China in this respect.)
- The ending of continued Chinese state intervention in industrial policy and explicit discriminatory restrictions, such as unlimited state funds for export financing and limitations on the level of foreign ownership in certain sectors.
- China's honoring its 2001 commitment to join the Agreement on Government Procurement (GPA) and engaging constructively in negotiations on opening its public procurement markets.
- The continuation of the rise in value of the renminbi, and the Chinese holding more exchange reserves in euros.
- The exploitation of the opportunities of China's emerging renewable energy sector for the European renewable energy business sector, and improving market access in this field.
- Enhanced cooperation to promote the transfer of low-carbon technology, in particular energy efficiency and renewables.
- An effective and efficient use of trade defense instruments, which contribute to ensuring fair conditions of trade between China and the EU.
- Working to overcome barriers to market economy status, to be granted only when China has fulfilled the criteria.
- The implementation and enforcement of IPRs and the continuation of the fight against counterfeiting.
- The need to reduce the high levels of pollution caused by China's industry and its growing consumption of natural resources, being aware of the shared European responsibility for the situation (given that a high share of Chinese industrial production is owned by European firms or ordered by European firms and retailers for consumption in Europe.)
- The maximization of efforts to eliminate child labor in China by removing the underlying causes.

and even if it were, China would understandably not accept the linkages between trade on the one hand and human rights, the environment, and social issues on the other.

The European Court of Justice

To some extent, the European Court of Justice (ECJ) is the EU's supreme court, with the responsibility to decide what is legal and what is not under the founding Treaties. Cases may be brought to the ECJ by the Commission, the European Parliament, member governments, nationals of member governments, or foreign entities. Given its powers to interpret the provisions of the European treaties, the ECJ has played an important role in implementing the EU's common commercial policy.

The ECJ has played a major role in deciding how policy powers are to be assigned between the Commission and member states in a number of issue areas. Known as the issue of 'competence', the ECJ has clarified that trade in goods falls within the exclusive competence of the EU, but that investment remains mainly within the competence of member states. And in 1994 the ECJ rejected the Commission's request to extend its competence for goods to services and intellectual property as well. By ruling that these were areas of mixed competence, thereby subject to the principle of unanimity, the ECJ arguably reduced the leverage of the

---

- The ratification by China of ILO Convention No. 87 on Freedom of Association and Protection of the Right to Organize, and the International Covenant on Civil and Political Rights.
- European businesses operating in China to apply the highest international standards and best practices in corporate social responsibility with regard to workers and the environment.
- Bringing working conditions in China up to the level of the core ILO standards.
- Cooperation on standards on cars, trucks, heavy vehicles, aviation and shipping, to lower greenhouse gas emissions and make the above-mentioned standards more climate-friendly.
- Cooperation on the regulation, evaluation and authorization of chemicals (REACH) between the EU and China.
- Cooperation on product safety, including trilateral contacts between the Commission, the US and the Chinese administrations, and the establishment of a joint working party on product and import safety within the Transatlantic Economic Council.

Commission vis-a-vis member states during internal bargaining on the EU position.[12]

III. The Decision-Making Process for the Imposition of Safeguard Measures

A safeguard investigation may be initiated by the Commission at its own initiative or at the request of one or more member states.[13] Prior to initiation, the Commission must consult the member states. The 'Safeguards Advisory Committee' used for this purpose tends to be staffed by the same government officials that also staff the Anti-Dumping and Anti-Subsidy Advisory Committees.

If, after consultations, the Commission considers that it has sufficient evidence, it will initiate an investigation. The opening of the investigation is published in the C series of the Official Journal.

Contrary to the practice set out under Regulation 288/82, the Commission now sends out questionnaires for producers and for exporters which will need to be completed by all interested parties. The Commission will also carry out verifications of selected questionnaire responses. Compared to anti-dumping/anti-subsidy questionnaires and verifications, the safeguard measure equivalents are relatively simple and straightforward.

The procedures for requesting a hearing by the Commission are contained in Article 6(4) of the Regulation. Thus, the Commission may hear the interested parties, but such parties must be heard where they have applied in writing, within the period laid down in the notice of initiation,

---

[12] Woolcock, S. (2000). European trade policy. In Helen Wallace and William Wallace (eds), *Policy-Making in the European Union*, Oxford University Press: Oxford, pp. 274–375.

[13] With respect to the provision, safeguard measures mandated by Commission Regulation (EC) No. 560/2002 of 27 March 2002, as amended by Commission Regulation (EC) No. 950/2002 of 3 June 2002, and Commission Regulation (EC) No. 1287/2002 of 15 July 2002, the investigation concerning certain steel products was initiated at the request of "several members states". With respect to the safeguard measures sanctioned by Commission Regulation (EC) No. 658/2004, the investigation concerning canned mandarins was initiated at the request of Spain and with respect to safeguard measures imposed through Commission Regulation No. 206/2005. The investigation concerning farmed salmon was initiated at the request of the UK and Ireland.

showing that they are actually likely to be affected by the outcome of the investigations and that there are special reasons for them to be heard orally.

Interested parties which make themselves known in time also have access to the non-confidential version of the information made available to the Commission by the complainants, provided for in Article 6(2).

IV. EU Trade Policy Making in the WTO Framework

The EU has a common trade policy ('Common Commercial Policy'). In other words, where trade, including WTO matters, is concerned, the EU acts as one single actor, for which the European Commission negotiates trade agreements and represents the European interests on behalf of the EU's 27 member states.

On this basis, the Commission negotiates on behalf of the member states, in consultation with the Article 133 Committee. The Committee is composed of representatives from the 27 member states and the European Commission. Its main function is to coordinate EU trade policy. The Committee meets on a weekly basis. It discusses the full range of trade policy issues affecting the Community, from strategic issues surrounding the launch of rounds of trade negotiations at the WTO to specific difficulties with the exports of individual products, and considers the trade aspects of wider Community policies in order to ensure consistency of policy. In this Committee, the Commission presents and secures endorsement of the member states on all trade policy issues. The major formal decisions (for example, an agreement to launch or conclude negotiations) are then confirmed by the Council of Ministers.

The WTO was established in 1995 as a result of the Uruguay Round of multilateral trade negotiations (1986–1994). It is an international organization that sets global rules of trade between nations. The core of the WTO system, referred to as the multilateral trading system, are the WTO agreements which lay down the legal ground rules for international trade, as well as the market-opening commitments taken up by its members.

The WTO is composed of governments and political entities (such as the EU) and is a member-driven organization, with decisions mainly taken on a consensus basis. Membership implies a balance of rights and obligations. Among some 150 WTO members, the largest and most comprehensive entity is the European Union with its 27 member states. Indeed, the EC has been a major player in the General Agreement on Tariffs and Trade (GATT) both before and after the creation of the WTO.

It is also one of the driving forces behind the multilateral trade negotiations in the WTO in relation to market opening and rule-making. The EU, together with the US, Japan and Canada, is one of the four major players of international trade law.[14]

The WTO's top-level decision-making body is the Ministerial Conference, which meets at least once every two years. Below this, the General Council meets several times a year in the Geneva headquarters of the WTO. Both are composed of representatives of all member states. At the next level, the Goods Council, Services Council and Intellectual Property Council as well as numerous specialized committees, working groups and working parties deal with the individual agreements and other areas such as the environment, development, membership applications and trade agreements. Finally, the WTO Secretariat in Geneva supplies technical support for various councils and committees and the ministerial conferences, analyzes world trade and explains WTO affairs to the public and media.

Trade negotiations under the WTO's auspices provide an example of how the EU trade policy-making mechanism operates in practice. The Commission sets and carries forward the priorities and aims of the EU as laid down in guidelines given by the Council of Ministers. Officials from the Commission's Directorate-General for Trade, under the authority of the Commissioner are charged with actually conducting the negotiations, and speak on behalf of the EU as a whole. Coordination with member states is assured at all times through the "133 Committee", while the Commission regularly keeps the Parliament informed. At the end of the round, the Council has to formally agree on the outcome.

V. Comments on the EU's Trade Policy-Making Mechanism

It is known that the EU's trade policy-making mechanism involves two levels of delegation. First, the 1957 Treaty of Rome formally transferred the competence to negotiate and conclude international agreements on trade in goods from the individual member states to the Community. It should be noted that the Community competence manifests itself at the negotiation stage (where the Commission acts upon a mandate agreed upon by

---

[14] Baroncini, E. (1998). The European community and the diplomatic phase of the WTO dispute settlement understanding. In P. Eeckhout and T. Tridimas (eds), *Yearbook of European Law,* Volume 18, Oxford University Press: New York.

the Council of Ministers), as well as at the ratification stage (where individual member states no longer have the power to formally ratify international engagements but instead delegate this power to the collective Council of Ministers). In other cases — mostly in transport, cultural, and educational services — trade policy is governed by the regime of 'mixed competence', which allows for parliamentary control at the national level.

The second level of delegation in the EU's trade policy is the practical transfer of competence from the Council of Ministers to the European Commission. The Commission elaborates on proposals for the initiation and content of international trade negotiations. The key policy discussions take place in the "133 Committee", which is composed of senior civil servants and trade experts from the member states as well as Commission representatives. The Committee examines and amends Commission proposals on a consensual basis, before transmitting them to the COREPER and subsequently the General Affairs Council (composed of foreign ministers from the member states), which then hands out a negotiating mandate to the Commission. In most cases, at least in theory, this mandate is agreed upon on a qualified majority basis. In practice, however, member states have always managed to reach consensus on a common text by this stage of the process, as with most other areas of policy-making in the EU. Commission officials representing the Union, under the authority of the Commissioner in charge of external economic affairs, conduct international trade negotiations within the limits set by the Council's mandate. While the member states coordinate their positions in Brussels and Geneva, the European Commission alone speaks for the EU at almost all WTO meetings. Member states are allowed to observe but not speak in WTO plenary sessions. At the conclusion of the negotiations, the Council approves or rejects the trade agreement.

It should also be pointed out that there are other factors that affect country-specific trade policies of the EU. The EU does not have specific trade agreements with its major trading partners among developed countries like the US and Japan. Trade is handled through the WTO mechanisms, although the EU has many agreements in individual sectors with both countries. However, while the WTO framework also applies to trade between the EU and China, China and the EU have worked together since 1975 in formulating a series of legal instruments to regulate trade relations between China and the EU. Specific bilateral trade agreements certainly play a role in the EU trade policy making towards China. Although the EU's trade policy in general is underpinned by its commitments to take measures necessary to integrate developing countries into the world trading system, notably by granting preferential trade treatment to less developed countries and strengthening assistance to build capacity,[15] its China policy is in stark contrast compared with its trade policy towards developing countries in general.

Last but not least, it should be mentioned that the institutional setting, member states and the dominant bureaucratic actors interplay and help shape EU trade policy making towards China. For example, member-state-centric approaches may mould the EU's trade policy-making process, and the self-interests of the bureaucratic decision makers may also leave their mark on the trade policy within the institutional constraints.[16]

VI. Concluding Remarks

From the perspective of institutional arrangements, the making of the EU's trade policy can appear relatively straightforward. The Commission has the power to propose new initiatives and the Council has the power to approve these. In making its decision, the Council relies heavily on the advice of the "133 Committee". It has been observed that the EU position in its overall orientation towards 'trade venues' has been largely shaped by the EU Commission.[17]

While the roles and functions of the relevant decision-making institutions are spelled out, the relative influence of the key actors — the Commission, the Council, and the "133 Committee" — on any specific issue is not easy to discern. Nor is it clear how each of these institutions reach agreement and why they may disagree with each other.

Moreover, the EU lacks formal and public mechanisms for taking advice and recommendations from the private sector. In principle, no

---

[15] One exception is in the area of trade defense instruments. No distinction whatsoever is made between less developed countries or developing countries in the application of trade defense measures. It seems to the EC that the level of development of a country can never be an excuse for unfairly traded or subsidized goods.

[16] Elsig, M. (2007). Delegation and Agency in EU Trade Policy Making: Bringing Brussels Back in, Swiss National Centre of Competence in Research, Working Paper No. 2007/21, available at http://phase1.nccr-trade.org/images/stories/publications/IP2/MElsig_NCCRWP_EUTrade.pdf (last accessed September 30, 2011).

[17] *Ibid.*

individuals, private companies, and industries are permitted to take part in the trade policy-making mechanism. Most of the EU's trade policy making is done informally and behind closed doors. However, many interest groups have a way of being heard in the trade policy-making process, either through formal consultation or informal lobbying.

Some of the stress in the China-EU trade relationship derives from an EU decision-making system that is slow, opaque, and lacking in clear lines of authority between the Commission and member states. Given that the EU process is unlikely to change as result of external criticism, Chinese policy makers face the challenge of trying to better understand how the process works and can be influenced.

CHAPTER 6

CHINA'S TRADE POLICY-MAKING MECHANISM

Chinese trade policies, including trade development strategy, its export and import regime, and trade liberalization reforms, have contributed to China's rise as a major trading power. This in turn has prompted debate about the nature of the country's trade policy-making process, which might be unduly influenced by trade disputes between China and its trade partners including the EU. This chapter sheds light on this complex question by examining the changing domestic forces shaping China's foreign trade relations.

I. Guiding Principles of the Trade Policy-Making Process and their Application

Principles that Impact Trade Policies

China has traditionally used principles to guide policy. For example, the five principles of peaceful coexistence have served as an important foundation in China's foreign policy since the 1950s.[1] Like other laws and regulations, China's Foreign Trade Law lays down the guiding principles for shaping and implementing China's foreign trade policies. According to

---

[1] According to China, settling international disputes peacefully is a fundamental principle of international law. Since the founding of the People's Republic of China, it has expressed on many occasions that international disputes should be resolved through peaceful consultations. The late Premier Zhou, for example, announced the position of the Chinese government in his speech on the Indochina question at the Geneva Conference in 1954: that disputes among Asian countries should be settled by peaceful consultations, rather than by the use of force or threat of the use of force. In the Asia-Africa Conference in April 1955, Premier Zhou pointed out that with the guarantee of the Five Principles of Peaceful Coexistence, one had no reason to believe that international disputes cannot be settled.

the Foreign Trade Law (FTL), the guiding principle for China's trade policy is of equality and mutual benefit.[2] This concept alludes to the fourth principle of China's principles of peaceful coexistence — equality and mutual benefit — through which the country has sought to augment its position in global affairs. In formulating its trade policy, China also attaches importance to the principle of reciprocity.[3]

Chinese Premier Wen Jiabao once further outlined the five principles for fair trade,[4] which offer a useful framework for understanding how China assesses its own trade prospects and how it may respond to future trade challenges. The following is an elaboration of China's five principles for fair trade.[5]

Mutual benefit and win-win result

The most frequently cited of the five principles, the mutual benefit principle, suggests that thinking broadly, one should take account of the other party's interests while pursuing one's own objectives. The 'win-win' concept represents the two basic tenets of China's current economic diplomacy: to assuage concerns about China's rise, and to secure important new markets abroad for Chinese companies.

The principle is advocated to soften concerns about China's economic rise by offering concrete opportunities for trade partners to share in China's growth. For instance, by allowing phased-in, tariff-free access to a targeted set of agricultural products under an 'early harvest' scheme, China helped calm the fears of Association of Southeast Asian Nations (ASEAN) members, many of which view China as a competitor, and precipitated an

---

[2] Article of the FTL: The state "shall, on the principle of equality and mutual benefit, promote and develop trade relations with other countries and regions, enter into or participate in such regional economic trade agreements as customs union agreements and free trade agreements, and participate in regional economic organizations".

[3] That is, to grant the other contracting parties or participating parties most-favored-nation treatment or national treatment in the field of foreign trade.

[4] (2003). 'Wen proposes principles on Sino-US trade, economic ties', *People's Daily*, December 9. http://english.peopledaily.com.cn/200312/09/eng20031209_129959.shtml (last accessed September 30, 2011).

[5] Sutter, K. M. (2006). China's "win-win" trade policy, *chinabusinessreview.com* September–October. http://www.hrs3.net/nfatc/readings/SutterKarenCommentary.pdf (last accessed September 30, 2011).

ASEAN-China Free-Trade Area (ACFTA) goods agreement. China is also promising investment and trade deals in infrastructure, agriculture, raw materials, energy, and tourism to win over newer trade partners such as Argentina, Australia, Brazil, Nigeria, and South Africa — and to divert attention away from swelling Chinese manufactured exports to those countries.

Finally, to protect itself from potential backlash and protectionism abroad, China has been seeking to foster growing economic interdependence to align itself with foreign companies and industries that have benefited from trade with China. Although the US has become familiar with this strategy over the years, it is new in other parts of the world, such as Australia, Brazil, and South Africa, where economic relations with China have recently deepened.

In these countries, diverging commercial interests have split the business communities vis-à-vis China, and potential fault lines on policy toward China are emerging.

Development first

This principle suggests that existing differences should be resolved through expanded trade and economic cooperation. With the guiding mantra of 'development first', China seeks to grow its way out of its trade surplus with the US, the EU and other trade partners through increased imports and buying missions, particularly during times of political and commercial tension. For instance, China timed the announcement of purchase of foreign goods, such as a US $45 billion purchase of US goods for the lead-up to Chinese President Hu Jintao's visit to Washington D.C. in January 2011, in an attempt to boost imports from the US and defuse tensions over the trade imbalance. In another move to increase imports, China announced plans to encourage domestic consumption as part of its 11th Five-Year Plan (2006–2010) and 12th Five-Year Plan (2011–2015).

However, such a policy requires time-consuming structural adjustments and, in the meantime, exports will likely remain an important engine of China's economic growth.

Consultative mechanisms

China attaches great importance to inter-government coordinating mechanisms in bilateral trade relations. Disputes should be addressed in a timely manner through communication and consultation to avoid possible escalation. The Chinese government has traditionally attached great importance to senior level dialogues as a way of smoothing bilateral trade relationships with other nations. This explains why following the formal establishment of the High Level Economic and Trade Dialogue between China and the EU in 2007, it created the ministerial-level position of Trade Representative in 2009 to handle high-profile disputes with its trade partners.

China has also established new bilateral and regional cooperation mechanisms with a host of foreign governments, including Argentina, Brazil, the EU, India, and South Korea, in order to resolve trade disputes promptly. A recent agreement to establish a China-ASEAN regional dispute resolution body could help China contain trade disputes within the region. Following allegations in 2004 — from both domestic media and neighbors such as Japan, South Korea, Taiwan, and Hong Kong — that Chinese beer and seafood contained unsafe additives, and after parasites were discovered in Chinese kimchi on the eve of the Asia-Pacific Economic Cooperation summit in November 2005, Beijing also negotiated a new bilateral forum on food standards with South Korea.

Equal consultation

This principle suggests that in trade relations, the two sides concerned should seek consensus while downplaying differences on major issues, instead of imposing restrictions or sanctions at every turn. Equal consultation, which stresses finding consensus on major issues, echoes an approach outlined by China's late Premier Zhou Enlai that served China well in resolving contentious diplomatic issues. Under this principle, China attempts to focus the attention of its trade partners on the benefits of the overall relationship in order to discourage the use of formal trade remedies, such as sanctions, and defuse trade tensions. In its dealings with the EU, for instance, China has highlighted its willingness to hold dialogues on human rights to demonstrate the importance of the broader bilateral relationship over contentious issues such as the trade imbalance. Under this approach, China has been much more willing since 2003 to acknowledge its trading partners' concerns about the trade deficit and renminbi revaluation as shared concerns, although it still remains slow to address them.

No politicization of trade issues

To keep trade disputes from spilling over into the political arena and thus deflate the demands of its trade partners, China often appeals to its trade partners to refrain from politicizing trade disputes. China tends to charge other countries with politicization if they push hard on trade disputes in a high-profile manner, indicating that this defensive tactic is an attempt to lower the profile of commercial tensions and prevent them from spoiling the broader political relationship.

> The core elements of these principles are development, equality, and mutual benefit. Development is our driving force, equality the premise, and mutual benefit our goal by putting development first, we mean to take a forward-looking approach that allows us to narrow the tradegap through continued expansion of two-way trade.[6]

Application of the Guiding Principles

China has shown that it can approach issues pragmatically on a case-by-case basis and emphasize selective aspects of principles for its own benefit during negotiations. However, China does not always appear to be consistently negotiating in true 'win-win' terms, and this principle at times seems to provide mere window dressing for Beijing's preferred *quid pro quo* approach to negotiations, especially regarding market access issues. Faced with pressure from major trade partners to implement WTO commitments and open markets further, China is working to ensure that it will get something in return for market access, even for commitments it has already agreed to implement. For instance, in response to challenges to its enforcement of intellectual property rights, China uses the 'win-win' principle to argue that it should not be burdened with heavy royalties and licensing fees as it tries to catch up in its own technological development. China also argues that countries should promote technology transfers and share the benefits of IP development more equitably so that developing countries can benefit from new technologies.

Nevertheless, the principles provide an important window into Beijing's current thinking and policy direction. Indeed, China's trade principles are an integral component of a broader effort to refashion China's foreign policy in an era of economic globalization, when its trade relationships are increasingly complex and difficult to balance. Such an approach not only shows that senior Chinese leaders recognize the potential magnitude of trade problems and the need to address the grievances of major

---

[6] (2003). Wen proposes ... *op.cit.*

trade partners, but also reveals the considerable challenges and constraints they face in managing these issues.

II. China's Institutional Framework for Trade Policy

China's Foreign Trade Law provides the institutional framework for the trade policies. The Foreign Trade Law is designed to oversee the opening up of the economy to the outside world, develop foreign trade, maintain order in foreign trade, protect the legitimate rights and interests of foreign trade dealers, and promote the sound development of the socialist market economy. The Foreign Trade Law requires the pursuit of a uniform foreign trade regime, the encouragement of development in foreign trade and the maintenance of fair and free foreign trade order. The Foreign Trade Law, which is very general by nature, is supplemented by the Regulations on the Import and Export of Merchandise Goods and Regulations on the Import and Export of Technology, passed in December 2001.[7] The two new regulations specifically define the general rules established by the Foreign Trade Law.

Numerous other new laws and regulations covering nearly all aspects of trading with China have been issued or have come into force, all with the purpose of fulfilling China's accession commitments. For example, on 1 January 2002, new customs regulations took effect. These aimed to clarify how Chinese customs authorities calculate import and export duties. The regulations also allow trading companies to apply for a ruling on classification up to three months before goods are imported or exported, waive tariffs, and temporarily simplify the process for importing goods.

The amended laws and revised regulations will be promulgated or issued after proper legal procedures are followed. In the meantime, provincial and local authorities are still reviewing their laws and regulations to see if they are consistent with national laws. Provincial-level laws, regulations, and other regulatory measures that implement the central government's legal measures are submitted to the central government for review.

Some trade partners have criticized China's intellectual property rights (IPR) protections as inadequate. Upon accession to the WTO, the Chinese

---

[7] They replaced previous laws and regulations regarding merchandise trade, such as the Provisional Procedures on Operating and Managing Import and Export Commodities, which was promulgated on 19 July 1994, and the Provisional Regulations on Managing the Import of Machinery and Electronic Products, which was promulgated on 7 October 1993.

government committed itself to the WTO Agreement on Trade-Related Aspects of Intellectual Property Rights (TRIPS Agreement), and began reviewing and amending China's intellectual property rights laws. China's amended Patent Law and its implementing rules, which took effect on 1 July 2001, streamline the patent application process, standardize patent infringement penalties, simplify enforcement procedures, and shift the burden of proof to defendants in patent infringement cases. Other IPR laws and regulations that address computer software, copyrights, trademarks, and criminal enforcement against counterfeiting were amended shortly thereafter. Some of the newly amended laws and regulations offer protection that is even more comprehensive than that offered in some developed economies. For example, the TRIPS Agreement contains no specific requirements regarding software infringement by end users; it is up to WTO members themselves to determine the obligations of end users. While most developed members define infringement as unauthorized commercial use, China's newly amended software regulations extend infringement penalties to unauthorized non-commercial use.

In addition to amending previous trade rules and principles and creating new ones, the Chinese government has issued a series of regulations concerning foreign investment liberalization and market access improvement in banking, insurance, telecommunications, distribution, consulting, and some other service sectors. To conform to WTO commitments on foreign investment, China revised its Catalogue Guiding Foreign Investment in Industry and its Regulations Guiding Foreign Investment, both of which took effect on 1 April 2002. More industries have accordingly been made open to wholly foreign-owned enterprises. New rules have eliminated the WTO-incompatible requirements on foreign exchange, forced transfer of advanced technology, export performance, and local content as conditions for investment by foreign-owned enterprises.

In July 2001, China's Ministry of Foreign Trade and Economic Cooperation (MOFTEC) began loosening restrictions on trading rights for domestic private enterprises when it issued its Circular Concerning the Rules Administering Trading Rights. The objective of this circular was to shift MOFTEC out of managing trade to simply registering prospective domestic traders. These rules extend trading rights to private manufacturing firms as well as to private trading companies. To improve transparency, the rules set time limits for the approval process, so that the regulatory authorities can no longer hold up applications indefinitely. The rules also reduced the minimum capital requirement for wholly Chinese-owned enterprises to obtain trading rights. In July 2001, MOFTEC issued its Circular Concerning the Extension of Trading Rights for Foreign-Owned Enterprises, which granted trading rights to some foreign-owned firms ahead of the schedule set forth in the Protocol.[8]

III. Agencies Involved in the Trade Policy-Making Process

According to the Foreign Trade Law, it is within the province of the "authority responsible for foreign trade under the State Council to administer the foreign trade of the entire country".[9] In other words, the Ministry of Commerce (MOFCOM) is in charge of administering foreign trade.

According to the State Council, the mission of the MOFCOM includes the following:

(1) To formulate development strategies, guidelines and policies of domestic and foreign trade and international economic cooperation, draft laws and regulations governing domestic and foreign trade, economic cooperation and foreign investment, devise implementation rules and regulations. To study and put forward proposals on harmonizing domestic legislations on trade and economic affairs as well as bringing Chinese economic and trade laws into conformity with multilateral and bilateral treaties and agreements.

…

(4) To study on and work out measures for the regulation of import and export commodities and compile a catalogue thereof, organize the implementation of import and export quota plan, decide on quota quantity and issue licenses; to draft and implement import and export commodity quota tendering policies.

(5) To formulate and execute policies concerning trade in technology, state import and export control, and policies encouraging the export of technology and complete set of equipment; to push forward the establishment of [a] foreign trade standardization system; to supervise technology import, equipment import, export of domestic technologies

---

[8] United States Trade Representative (2002). National Trade Estimate Report on Foreign Trade Barriers (NTE), available at http://www.ustraderep.gov/Document_Library/Reports_Publications/2002/2002_NTE_Report/Section_Index.html (last accessed October 10, 2011).

[9] Article 3 of the Foreign Trade Law.

subject to state export restriction and re-export of imported technologies, and to issue export licenses pertaining to nuclear non-proliferation.

(6) To study, put forth and implement multilateral and bilateral trade and economic cooperation policies, be responsible for multilateral and bilateral negotiations on trade and economic issues, coordinate domestic positions in negotiating with foreign parties, and to sign the relevant documents and monitor their implementation ... To handle major issues in country-specific economic and trade relationships, regulate trade and economic activities with countries without diplomatic [relations] with China. In line with the mandate, to handle the relationship with the World Trade Organization on behalf of the Chinese government, undertake such responsibilities under the framework of the WTO as multilateral and bilateral negotiations, trade policy reviews, dispute settlement, and notifications and inquires.

...

(8) To organize and coordinate the work pertaining to [anti-dumping], countervailing, safeguard measures and other issues related to fair trade for import and export. To institute a fair trade early warning mechanism for import and export, and organize industry injury investigations. To guide and coordinate domestic efforts in responding to foreign [anti-dumping], countervailing, and safeguard investigations and other issues concerned.

(9) To give general guidance to nationwide efforts in foreign investment ... To draw up and enforce foreign investment policies and reform schemes, participate in the formulation of mid-term and long-term planning and development strategies for foreign investment utilization. To examine and approve, according to relevant laws, the establishment and changes thereafter of [foreign-owned] enterprises with foreign input exceeding the state fixed amount, or engaged in restricted business areas, or in businesses subject to quota and license administration. To verify the contracts and statutes of large-scale projects with foreign investment and their major subsequent changes, particularly stipulated in relevant [legislation]. To supervise the enforcement of laws, regulations, contracts and statutes by [foreign-owned] enterprises. To guide and oversee nationwide efforts in attracting foreign investment and other business opportunities, as well as the establishment and trade performance of [foreign-owned] enterprises in China. Comprehensively guide and coordinate the specific work of state-level economic and technological development zones.[10]

...

---

[10] http://english.mofcom.gov.cn/mission.shtml (last accessed September 30, 2011).

However, other agencies can also have their voice heard in formulation of China's foreign trade policy.

First, the MOFCOM is part of the State Council. While the MOF-COM administers trade policies under the auspices of the latter, the State Council headed by the Prime Minister is the *de facto* decision maker in the area of key foreign trade policies. Given the Chinese Communist Party (CCP) exercises a monopoly on political power, the CCP Central Committee and Politburo are at the top of the decision-making hierarchy. Secondly, other relevant ministries can influence the trade policy-making process. In this sense, the MOFCOM is no more than a coordinating body or even *primus inter pares* in the formulation of trade policies that involve both the MOFCOM and other ministries. These relevant ministries include the National Development and Reform Commission (NDRC), the Ministry of Agriculture, and the Ministry of Industries and Information Technology (MIIT). Where the trade policy concerns industrial policy, it is the NDRC that is primarily the primary decision maker.[11] When it comes to trade in agricultural products, it is primarily within the domain of the Ministry of Agriculture.[12] When it comes to the information industry or raw material industries or equipment industry, the MIIT plays a key role.[13]

Thirdly, the legislature of China has its say in the formation of trade treaties or agreements, which form the legal foundations for China's trade

---

[11] For example, the NDRC played a key role in the adoption of the Foreign Investment Catalogue in 2007, which suggested a more selective approach to foreign investment, targeting higher value-added sectors rather than basic manufacturing. It includes new restricted sectors such as biofuel production and soy crushing, and blanket prohibitions on foreign investment in movie production, news websites, and audiovisual and Internet services.

[12] It is within the mandate of the Ministry of Agriculture to "undertake foreign-related agricultural affairs". http://english.agri.gov.cn/ga/amoa/mandates/ (last accessed September 30, 2011).

[13] The MIIT is responsible for regulation and development of raw material industries, the equipment industry, the Internet, wireless, broadcasting, communications, production of electronic and information goods, software industry and the promotion of the national knowledge economy. The MIIT is found to issue government 'opinions' that calls for expanded domestic market share in industrial machinery manufacturing sectors. These opinions could pose difficulties for foreign investors seeking control of leading domestic firms.

policy, or at least the main part of China's trade policy. Indeed, the MOF-COM is responsible for negotiating trade treaties and agreements under the auspices of the State Council. However, pursuant to the Constitution of the People's Republic of China, it is within the purview of the Standing Committee of the National People's Congress to ratify treaties and other important agreements.

Fourthly, thanks to gradual political democratization and fast economic growth, more diversified social interests become virtually legitimate and active in a corporatist state, consequently leading to increased lobbying and rent-seeking activities for import protection and export preferential trade policies. Lobbying patterns in China are becoming more open and pluralistic. Central executive agencies, sectoral interests, regional interests, and even transnational actors are increasingly able to influence the process and outcome of China's trade policy making. It has been found that the bureaucracy in central executive bodies and local governments, favored in 'clientelism' network culture, appear to be a dominant interest group, while others, mainly composed of domestic enterprises of various kinds, foreign investors, and consumers, only have a marginal or diminishing impact on decision making.[14] Such an observation can be demonstrated by several case studies, including but not limited to policies protecting the telecommunications sector, import quotas and license requirements, export quota bidding, foreign exchange retention and multiple exchange rates, anti-dumping enforcement and the anti-smuggling campaign.

In conclusion, as a result of national reforms, although trade policy-making has been highly centralized in MOFCOM, which reports directly to the State Council, other regulatory agencies have become more involved. While interest groups, varying from national regulatory agencies, state-owned enterprises (SOEs) and other 'national champions' in the private sector (or with hybrid forms of ownership), state-sponsored trade associations, as well as provincial and municipal governments, proliferate and have an increasing stake in China's trade with its partners, the government faces more lobbying and resistance to further liberalization. Economic nationalism as a force in government and the CCP is more influential than it was in the 1990s, though not quite in the driver's seat.

---

[14] Sheng Bin (2002). *The Political Economy of China's Foreign Trade Policy*, Sanlian: Shanghai.

IV. The Issue of Transparency in China's Trade Policy-Making and Implementing Mechanism

There are quite a few issues in China's trade policy-making and implementing mechanism. While there is notably a risk of politicizing trade issues, this chapter will only focus on the issue of transparency.

Transparency is an oft-criticized issue in China's trade policy-making and implementing mechanism. China has committed to transparency obligations set forth by the WTO Agreement and the Protocol on the Accession of the People's Republic of China (the Accession Protocol). For example, as a condition to its accession, China agreed that only published or readily available laws, regulations, and other measures pertaining to or affecting goods, services, trade-related aspects of intellectual property rights, and the control of foreign exchange (collectively referred to as 'measures') shall be enforced. China also undertook to make information on these measures available to WTO members on request, before these measures are actually implemented. In emergency situations, trade rules must be made available no later than their entry into force or implementation at the latest when they are implemented or enforced. In addition, China was required to construct enquiry points to provide information about measures on goods, trade-related aspects of intellectual property rights, and foreign exchange control.

China's WTO Accession Protocol required it to provide a comment period prior to the adoption of any measure affecting trade in goods and services, trade-related aspects of intellectual property rights, or foreign exchange control. References to this general obligation are also contained in the Working Party Report on China's WTO accession. China's legal obligation in this regard provides businesses and other interested parties with opportunities to comment on the drafting of China's trade policies.[15]

Despite this, one would be naive to think that China will be free from accusation in the area of transparency with regard to the making and implementation of its trade policies.

V. Implications of China's Trade-Policy Making Mechanism for China-EU Trade Relations

The successful implementation of the five principles ultimately depends on China's continued economic growth and demand for foreign goods and

---

[15] Wang, H. (2010). Enhancing business participation in trade policy-making: Lessons from China. In Debra Stegar (ed), *Redesigning the World Trade Organization for the Twenty-first Century*, Wilfrid Laurier University Press: Canada.

services. The specific commercial benefits that China brings to the table, such as new trade and investment opportunities for southern Europe and Latin America and strong demand from China's raw materials and commodities sectors, have given Premier Wen's trade approach more credence among China's trade partners.

Whether China will succeed in mitigating trade conflicts remains to be seen. Like other countries, China has a small trade negotiation team that is increasingly stretched across a wide range of issue areas. As the number and scope of China's trade negotiations increase, it will be more difficult to keep up with the demands of these relationships. China's preference for conceding as little as possible in negotiations may also hinder its ability to contain disputes, especially if it miscalculates the political pressures involved. China also has pockets of domestic resistance to a trade approach that not only seeks to accommodate the interests of its trade partners, but also threatens industrial policies and export platforms that benefit constituents at home (see p. 42). Chinese Minister of Commerce Bo Xilai has shown a willingness to play to domestic stakeholders such as the textile industry, and the PRC National Development and Reform Commission has recently responded to industry concerns about growing foreign strength in manufacturing sectors such as auto and construction equipment.

Despite the potential limits of the 'win-win' approach, China will likely keep using these five trade principles to soften opposition to China's economic rise and prevent commercial disputes from spilling over into the political arena. China's growth depends heavily on its exports and requires strong political relationships with major developed and developing countries. Recognizing the limits of its ability to ward off future safeguard and antidumping actions, China will likely try to avoid a broad-based global attack on its trade practices. However, the road ahead for China could be rocky, and it will come under intense pressure over its management of economic relations, given the extent of its commercial exposure and the steady demands on Beijing to translate promises into reality.

CHAPTER 7

TRANSITIONAL PRODUCT-SPECIFIC SAFEGUARD MEASURES AND THEIR IMPLICATION FOR TRADE DISPUTES BETWEEN CHINA AND THE EU

I. Introduction

This chapter draws on the conflict over the EU's transitional product-specific safeguard mechanism for imports originating in China.

Transitional product-specific safeguard measures (TPSSMs) refer to the restrictive trade measures adopted by any WTO member, for the purpose of protection of its domestic industry for a specific period of time under the WTO transitional product-specific mechanism to prevent the increase of imported products originating in a specific country. In contrast with the unlimited term of the application of the Agreement on Safeguards, the term of application is limited. As such, TPSSMs are transitional.

In a sense, the nature of TPSSMs is heavily influenced by Section 406 of the Trade Act of the United States. TPSSMs were first applied against Japan when it applied for membership of the General Agreement on Tariffs and Trade (GATT) in 1953. Under the provisions agreed between Japan and the GATT Contracting Parties, any other GATT contracting party had the right to unilaterally adopt measures to protect its domestic industry from the damage incurred by the market disruption as a consequence of an increase in imports of textile products originating in Japan.

The TPSSMs against China are generally considered as "a result of the perception of China as a non-market economy from the standpoint of some developed countries".[1] During the negotiations concerning China's

---

[1] Jin X. (2010). A Preliminary Probe into the Product-specific Safeguard Measures Against China, available at http://article.chinalawinfo.com/Article_Detail.asp?ArticleId=36842 (last accessed September 30, 2011).

accession to the WTO, the US pressured China to agree to the provisions of "Product-specific Safeguard Measures". China adopted a pragmatic and flexible attitude towards the negotiations for the sake of long-term trade relations with the outside world. China sought to accede to the WTO based on the consideration of a long-term strategy.

In November 1999, an agreement was reached between China and the US on the terms of China's accession to the WTO, in which the provision on TPSSMs was included. When China acceded to the WTO in 2001, the TPSSM provision was integrated in the Protocol on the Accession of the People's Republic of China. Therefore, in a sense, the provision of TPSSMs is the direct reflection of the trade interests of the US and other Western countries.

The TPSSMs provision, though very unfair to China and a violation of the principle of fair and liberal trade, is also "an option made by China under the premise of balancing advantages and disadvantages".[2] In general, the inclusion of the TPSSMs is a result of balancing trade interests and political compromise between China and its trade partners.

II. The EU's Transitional Product-Specific Safeguard Measures

The TPSSMs directed against China's products are mainly contained in Paragraph 16 of the Protocol on the Accession of the People's Republic of China (hereinafter referred to as the Accession Protocol). According to Paragraph 16 of the Accession Protocol, within the 12 years after China's accession to the WTO, in cases where products of Chinese origin are being imported into the territory of any WTO member in such increased quantities or under such conditions as to cause or threaten to cause market disruption to the domestic producers of like or directly competitive products, the WTO member thus affected may request consultations with China with a view to seeking a mutually satisfactory solution, including whether the affected WTO member should pursue application of a measure under the Agreement on Safeguards. If consultations do not lead to an agreement between China and the WTO member concerned within 60 days of the receipt of a request for consultations, the WTO member affected shall be free, with respect to such products, to withdraw concessions or otherwise limit imports only to the extent necessary to prevent or remedy such market disruptions.

---

[2] *Ibid.*

Immediately after China's entry into the WTO, quite a few WTO members made or modified their domestic laws on the basis of Paragraph 16 of the Accession Protocol in an effort to legitimatize the adoption of TPSSMs against products originating in China by means of domestic legislation. In the US, Section 421 was enacted as one element of 2,000 laws that aimed to implement a China-specific safeguard mechanism in China's WTO Accession Protocol that may be utilized by WTO members until December 2013. Section 421 authorizes the President to impose safeguards — that is, temporary measures such as import surcharges or quotas — on Chinese goods if any domestic market disruption is discovered. On the EU side, Council Regulation (EC) No. 427/2003 was adopted on 8 March 2003. The Regulation, named 'Transitional Product-specific Safeguard Mechanism for Imports Originating in China', is intended to reflect China's Accession Protocol, containing the terms and conditions for Chinese membership of the WTO, including the provision of a product-specific safeguard clause. The Regulation covers any imports entering the EU from China.

It is important to note that the Regulation covers two situations: it provides for the adoption of a safeguard measure where any specific imported Chinese product (a) causes or threatens to cause "market disruption", or (b) causes or threatens to cause "significant trade diversions" into the Community. Whether or not a market disruption is imminent or in existence will depend on a number of factors which the Commission will investigate. These include three factors in particular: the volume of the imports concerned; the effect of such imports on Community prices for like or directly competitive products; and the effect of such imports on the Community industry producing like or directly competing products.

A "significant trade diversion" is defined as an action by China or another WTO member taken to prevent or remedy market disruption on their territory, but which thereby creates a diversion of the trade, and a subsequent increase in imports, of a product from the China into the Community. The "action" will usually be a safeguard measure. The economic factors which the Commission is required to examine are the actual or imminent increase in market share of Chinese imports, the nature or extent of the action taken or proposed by China or other WTO members, the actual or imminent increase in the volume of Chinese imports due to such action taken or proposed, conditions of demand and supply in the Community surrounding the product under investigation, and the extent of exports from the China to the WTO member(s) applying a safeguard measure.

The TPSSM Regulation stipulates that a safeguard investigation can be initiated by the Commission, on its own initiative or by request of a member state. The Commission has to take into account trends in imports of the product under investigation, and analyze any available evidence pertaining to the economic factors outlined above. It must also announce its intention to initiate an investigation to the Chinese authorities, and may accompany this with an invitation for consultations. If it eventually does initiate an investigation, the Commission must ensure that, unless there is good cause, it is not initiated less then one year after the completion of a previous investigation.

The investigation is similar to that in anti-dumping proceedings. The Commission has given itself the power under the Regulation to carry out on-the-spot verifications, conduct oral hearings and ensure that any investigation is concluded within the normal time frame of nine months, unless exceptional circumstances warrant an extended period. Provisional measures may also be applied in "critical circumstances", i.e., where any delay would cause damage which would be difficult to repair, based on findings by the Commission. Member states should normally be consulted, but provisional measures may be taken in cases of extreme urgency, and the member states informed of them later on. The measures can take the form of customs duties and quantitative restrictions on imports from China, and they must not last longer than 200 days.

The EU may also decide, at the conclusion of an investigation, to impose definitive measures. Consultations with the Chinese authorities will be necessary beforehand. Measures can be made to apply to imports entering any of the member states, or only one or more of them. However, if the measure is to be regional, it will have to be temporary, and must ensure non-disruption of the internal market.

While a safeguard measure has to be lifted as soon as the trade situation to which it applies has been remedied, the period of application shall not exceed four years. Nonetheless, this period may be extended if it is felt that the measure continues to be necessary, and there is evidence that Community producers are adjusting. The new Regulation also allows for a suspension of a measure for nine months, or longer if necessary.

The Regulation fortunately stipulates that, so long as a quota is applied with regard to any particular products of Chinese origin, then such products cannot be the target of safeguard and trade diversion measures while the quota is in force.

The Regulation, which entered into force on 9 March 2003, will expire on 11 December 2013. Only after that date will quotas not be applied on products of Chinese origin.

III. An Overview of Transitional Product-Specific Safeguard Measures

General Safeguard Measures Under the GATT and the WTO

Article XIX of the General Agreement on Tariffs and Trade 1994 (GATT 1994) and the WTO Agreement on Safeguards permit WTO members to apply safeguards — that is, to temporarily suspend GATT tariff concessions or other GATT obligations owed to other WTO members — in order to remedy serious injury to domestic industries caused by surges of imported products from other WTO member countries. Section 1(a) of Article XIX states that if, as a result of unforeseen developments and of the effect of the obligations incurred by a contracting party under this Agreement, including tariff concessions, any product is being imported into the territory of that contracting party in such increased quantities and under such conditions as to cause or threaten serious injury to domestic producers in that territory of like or directly competitive products, the contracting party shall be free, in respect of such product, and to the extent and for such time as may be necessary to prevent or remedy such injury, to suspend the obligation in whole or in part or to withdraw or modify the concession.

Safeguard measures that were established in GATT Article XIX were then incorporated into the present WTO system through the WTO Agreement on Safeguards, with significant modifications. The Agreement on Safeguards expands on Article XIX, providing that safeguards may only be imposed if the importing member has conducted an investigation to determine if the conditions for imposing a safeguard have been met. It also states that a WTO member may not "take or seek any emergency action on particular products as set forth in Article XIX of the GATT 1994 unless such action conforms with the provisions of this Article as applied in accordance with this Agreement". The Agreement on Safeguards adds that the increased quantities of imports that are a prerequisite of a finding of serious injury may be "absolute or relative to domestic production".[3]

---

[3] The Agreement also sets out requirements for domestic safeguards investigations and for determinations of serious injury made in the course of such investigations. In addition, a WTO member imposing a safeguard is subject to detailed obligations to notify the WTO Committee on Safeguards and the WTO Council on Trade in Goods, and to consult with other affected WTO members.

The Agreement on Safeguards adds another requirement on the application of safeguards by providing that "[s]afeguard measures shall be applied to a product being imported irrespective of its source". There is no such requirement that disregards a product's origin in Article XIX of the GATT 1947, and its addition evinces the principle of non-discrimination that underpins the whole WTO system.

The "serious injury" standard contained in Article XIX and carried forward in the Safeguards Agreement is defined in the Agreement to be "a significant overall impairment in the position of a domestic industry".[4]

The Safeguards Agreement makes it clear that an Article XIX safeguard must be applied on a non-discriminatory basis, that is, it must be applied to the product at issue regardless of its source.

An Overview of Paragraph 16 of China's WTO Accession Protocol

Paragraph 16 of Part I of China's WTO Accession Protocol incorporated the 'Transitional Product-Specific Safeguard Mechanism'. It may be invoked by a WTO member "in cases where products of Chinese origin are being imported into the territory of … [the] member in such increased quantities or under such condition as to cause or threaten to cause market disruption to the domestic producers of like or directly competitive products".

The TPSSM contains both substantive and procedural requirements. According to the provisions of Paragraph 16 of the Accession Protocol, the application of TPSSMs must observe the following procedure:

Investigation

Investigation is the most basic method of truth finding. An action to address market disruption would be taken only after an investigation by the importing WTO member, pursuant to procedures previously established and made

---

[4] The WTO Appellate Body has found that this standard is "on its face, very high" or "exacting", particularly when compared with the "material injury" standard contained in the WTO Anti-dumping Agreement, the Agreement on Subsidies and Countervailing Measures, and Article VI of the GATT. Appellate Body Report (2001). *United States — Safeguard Measures on Imports of Fresh, Chilled or Frozen Lamb Meat from New Zealand and Australia,* paragraph 124, WT/DS177/AB/R, WT/DS178/AB/R (1 May).

available to the public. Investigation will be conducted on the import volume and market share of Chinese products and the effects of the imports on prices and the domestic industry of the importing country, as well as the existence of any causal link between the imports and market disruption.

Public notice and notification

To make the whole procedure fair and transparent, the importing member has to publish notice of the commencement of any investigation, any measure proposed to be taken, the decision to apply a measure, and the commencement of any process to consider the duration of the action. The Committee on Safeguards shall be notified immediately on any such action by China against the complainant or vice versa.

Consultations

(i)   Initiation of consultations. When products of Chinese origin are being imported into any WTO member state in such increased quantities or under such conditions as to cause or threaten to cause market disruption to the domestic producers of like or directly competitive products, the WTO member so affected may request consultations with China. The affected WTO member should pursue application of a measure under the Agreement on Safeguards.

(ii)   An agreement is reached. If these bilateral consultations lead to an agreement that imports of Chinese origin are a cause of market disruption, China shall take necessary action to prevent or remedy the market disruption.

(iii)   If consultations do not lead to an agreement between China and the WTO member concerned within 60 days of the receipt of a request for consultations, the WTO member affected has the right, in respect of such products, to withdraw concessions or otherwise to limit imports, but only to the extent necessary to prevent or remedy such market disruption.

Provisional safeguard measures

In a case where delay would cause damage that would be difficult to repair, the WTO member may implement a provisional safeguard measure pursuant to a preliminary determination that imports have caused or threatened to cause market disruption. In this case, notification of these measures should be made to the Committee on Safeguards and a request for bilateral consultations shall be effected immediately thereafter. The duration of the provisional measure shall not exceed 200 days and it shall be counted in the duration of the safeguard measures if the final determination is and affirmative and safeguard measures are necessary.

Retaliation

A WTO member shall apply a measure only for such a period of time as may be necessary to prevent or remedy the market disruption. China cannot retaliate in response to the application of TPSSMs unless a measure is taken based on a relative increase in imports for more than two years or an absolute increase in imports for more than three years.

From the point of view of substantive provisions, the TPSSM in the Accession Protocol defines "market disruption" as occurring whenever imports of an article, like or directly competitive with an article produced by the domestic industry, are increasing rapidly, either absolutely or relatively, so as to be a significant cause of material injury or threat of material injury to the domestic industry.

In determining whether market disruption exists, the importing member must look at "objective factors", including import volume, the effect of imports on prices for like or directly competitive articles, and the effect of the imports on the domestic industry producing such articles. As explained earlier, the "material injury" standard is considered less severe than the "serious injury" standard contained in the Article XIX of the GATT and the Agreement on Safeguards.

The safeguard may be applied only to goods of Chinese origin, a significant difference from the WTO Safeguards Agreement, which requires that a safeguard be imposed on the subject product regardless of its source. Although Paragraph 16.6 of the Accession Protocol allows a safeguard to be imposed "only for such period of time as may be necessary to prevent or remedy the market disruption", the Accession Protocol differs from the Safeguards Agreement in that it does not limit the duration of the measure. Similar to Article XIX of the GATT and the Safeguards Agreement, Paragraph 16.7 of the Accession Protocol permits the importing WTO member to apply a provisional safeguard measure, after it makes a preliminary determination that market disruption exists, where there are "critical circumstances", that is, where "delay would cause damage which it would be difficult to repair".

IV. A Chinese Perception of Transitional Product-Specific Safeguard Measures

In this regard, it is useful to evaluate the TPSSMs from the Chinese perspective.

The conditions for the application of TPSSMs are not well clarified and defined. According to Paragraph 16 of the Accession Protocol, the pre-conditions for the application of TPSSMs are the occurrence of an absolute or relative increase of the import of products originating in China, which has brought about market disruption, threat of market disruption or significant diversion of trade. Market disruption is considered to occur if the import of a Chinese product increases in such a manner, either absolutely or relatively, so as to constitute a significant cause of a material injury or a threat of material injury to the domestic industry of the importing country that produces like or directly competitive products. The problem is that there is no clear-cut definition or clarification of what may constitute significant diversion of trade, material injury or threat of material injury in the Accession Protocol. Furthermore, the standards set for the application of TPSSMs and the determination of material injury or threat of material injury are much lower that those set for serious injury or threat of serious injury to the domestic industry in the case of investigations for safeguards. Additionally, the fact that the material injury or threat of material injury is a significant cause rather than a major cause of injury to the domestic industry has lowered the baselines for the application of TPSSMs, as the importing country only has to prove that a product from China has increased in large numbers to apply TPSSMs.

The application of TPSSMs is selective and discriminatory. In sharp contrast with the principle of non-discrimination in the Safeguard Agreement, the application of TPSSMs is characterized by strong discrimination against China. The safeguards are the embodiment of the principle of change of circumstances applying to all WTO members and are "a safety valve ensuring domestic economic security of the WTO members and trade liberalization". The safeguards conform to and are themselves part of the set of WTO rules, and are thus lawful and non-discriminatory. However, TPSSMs were designed only to target products originating from China. Any WTO member can initiate the application of limits to the import of Chinese products if it can show that the import has caused the existence or threat of market disruption. Worse than that, against what products and when TPSSMs will be adopted are purely at the discretion of the importing country, which often results in discriminatory selection of products.

China is given limited rights to appeal against the adoption of TPSSMs. Paragraph 16 of the Accession Protocol provides that China has the right to suspend the application of substantially equivalent concessions or obligations under the GATT 1994 under two circumstances: when a measure that is taken as a result of a relative increase in the level of imports remains in effect more than two years, and when a measure that is taken as a result of an absolute increase in imports remains in effect more than three years. According to the Safeguard Agreement, the WTO member can adopt measures for retaliation at any time after the safeguard measures come into effect. Therefore the provision of TPSSMs has in fact limited the right of China to adopt retaliatory measures.

In general, the TPSSMs are identified as one of the four unfair provisions that China was forced to accept upon its accession to the WTO. Undoubtedly, the existence of TPSSMs encourages other WTO members to apply or even abuse safeguard measures against China, and forces Chinese enterprises into unfavorable conditions in which they face even more challenges. As pointed out by a scholar, it is highly doubtful whether it is justifiable to apply a safeguard measure based on anything less than serious injury to domestic industry.[5]

However, it should be pointed out that the acceptance of the provision was also a strategic option that China made in the process of trade negotiations in exchange for other concessions on other issues from other WTO members, such as intellectual property rights, where China has met strong setbacks. As such, TPSSMs were a result of combining strategic advancement and tactical compromise in tackling the balance of China's trade conflicts with its trade partners. Moreover, a careful study of trade development after China's accession indicates that the TPSSMs have not been used as often as they could have been.

---

[5] Lee, Y.S. (2002), The specific safeguard mechanism in the protocol on China's accession to the WTO: A serious step backward from the achievement of the Uruguay round. *Journal of World Intellectual Property*, 5, p. 227.

However, this does not mean that the TPSSMs do not constitute any negative influence on China's economy.

The TPSSMs may injure and threaten to injure Chinese domestic industries. The TPSSMs were first designed to protect the importing (applying) countries' domestic industries, which themselves may threaten or injure China's domestic industries. The application of TPSSMs will reduce the market share and production of Chinese products, thus causing a chain reaction that would injure the whole industry. China has a competitive edge in exporting textiles, but the existence and application of TPSSMs and quota limits have actually impeded the improvement of its textile industry.

The exports of relevant products may be negatively affected, which may result in the reduction of the profits of Chinese enterprises. The application of TPSSMs may lead directly to sharp limitations on the export of Chinese products, which may reduce the profits of the enterprise as a result. These enterprises will then be faced with four options: to stop their exports to the applying country, to adopt measures to cope with the TPSSMs, to seek to develop new markets, or to increase the technical content and added values of the export products. Whatever measures adopted, the affected enterprises will directly or indirectly suffer heavy losses as a result of the huge increase of their production costs caused by the limitations and challenges imposed on them by TPSSMs.

The TPSSMs constitute damage to fair competition and set back the process of economic development. Trade liberalization and fair competition have long been recognized as a major principle of international trade. The provision and the application of TPSSMs have violated the above-mentioned principle and are detrimental to the creation of a fair and competitive context for international trade. On the other hand, the TPSSMs are designed to target Chinese exports of products and exert a negative effect on China's economic growth. With the increase of China's economic influence, this will affect the stability and development of the world economy.

In a nutshell, the TPSSMs distort the principle of free and fair trade and have a far-reaching bearing upon China. Regarding their influence, the effect of TPSSMs must be reviewed from microscopic and macroscopic perspectives. In terms of macroscopic consideration, China's trade policy and trade regime will be affected, while the microscopic effect is reflected in the operations of enterprises and the development of domestic industries.

V. A Test of the TPSSM in the WTO

TPSSMs in the WTO

Until now, the EU has not yet initiated any TPSSMs. The only case of TPSSMs being used against Chinese products was by the US in September 2009.[6] However, more TPSSMs are expected to occur against the backdrop of the global financial crisis. In this connection, it is important to extrapolate the effects of the use of TPSSMs on China. Before commenting on the implication of the EU's use of TPSSMs, it is useful to examine the China-US dispute over the US's use of TPSSMs against imports of China-made tires.[7]

On 20 April 2009, the United Steel, Paper and Forestry, Rubber, Manufacturing, Energy, Allied Industrial and Service Workers International Union filed a petition with the US International Trade Commission (USITC) requesting an investigation under Section 421 of the Trade Act of 1974, 19 U.S.C. § 2451, a trade remedy statute addressing import surges from China, to examine whether Chinese passenger vehicle and light truck tires were causing market disruption to US tire producers. Market disruption will be found to occur under Section 421 whenever imports of a Chinese product that is "like or directly competitive with" a domestic product "are increasing rapidly [...] so as to be a significant cause of material injury, or threat of material injury, to the domestic industry". The ITC initiated the investigation (TA-421–7) on 24 April 2009.

As a result of its investigation, the ITC in June 2009 voted 4–2 that imports of the above-mentioned tires were causing domestic market disruption and recommended that the President impose an additional duty on these items for three years at an annually declining rate. The ITC also recommended expedited consideration of trade adjustment assistance applications filed by affected firms or workers. On 11 September 2009, President Obama proclaimed increased tariffs on Chinese tires for three years effective from 26 September 2009, albeit at lower rates than those

---

[6] Six petitions had been filed under Section 421 in the past, with the ITC finding that market disruption existed in four out of six of its investigations. However, President Bush had decided not to provide import relief in these earlier cases.

[7] Baroncini, E. (1998). The European community and the diplomatic phase of the WTO dispute settlement understanding. In P. Eeckhout and T. Tridimas (eds), *Yearbook of European Law*, Volume 18. Oxford University Press: New York.

recommended by the ITC. The tariff increase was set at 35% *ad valorem* in the first year, 30% in the second year, and 25% in the third year.

On 14 September 2009, China requested consultations with the US concerning these tariffs.[8] Despite that, the USITC determined that there was market disruption as a result of rapidly increasing imports of these tires from China, which was a significant cause of material injury to the domestic industry. Following a Presidential decision, these duties took effect as planned on 26 September 2009.

China argued that the higher tariffs were inconsistent with the national treatment obligation under Article I(1) of the GATT 1994 and were not properly justified pursuant to Article XIX of the GATT 1994 and the Agreement on Safeguards. China also maintained that these measures were not properly justified as China-specific restrictions under Paragraph 16 of its Protocol of Accession.[9]

---

[8] On 9 December 2009, China requested the establishment of a panel. At its meeting on 21 December 2009, the DSB deferred the establishment of a panel. At its meeting on 19 January 2010, the DSB established a panel pursuant to the request from China. The European Union, Japan, Chinese Taipei, Turkey and Viet Nam reserved their third-party rights. On 2 March 2010, China requested the Director-General to determine the composition of the panel was composed. On 12 March 2010, the panel was composed. On 31 May 2010, the Chairman of the panel informed the DSB that the panel would not be able to complete its work in six months in light of scheduling conflicts. On 8 November 2010, the final report was issued to the parties. On 13 December 2010, the panel report was circulated to members.

[9] China specifically alleged that

- the US statute defines "significant cause" more narrowly than required by the ordinary meaning of that phrase as used in Paragraph 16.4 of the Protocol of Accession;
- Paragraphs 16.1 and 16.4 was being violated by the US because (a) imports from China were not "in such increased quantities" and were not "increasing rapidly"; (b) imports from China were not a "significant cause" of material injury or threat thereof; and (c) the domestic tire producers were not experiencing "market disruption" or "material injury";
- Paragraph 16.3 was being violated by the US because the restrictions were being imposed beyond the "extent necessary to prevent or remedy" any alleged market disruption; and
- Paragraph 16.6 was being violated by the US because the restrictions were being imposed for a period of time longer than "necessary to prevent or remedy" any alleged market disruption.

China made seven specific claims in this dispute based on Paragraph 16 of the Protocol and GATT 1994. With respect to the Protocol, China asked the panel to determine if:

 (i)   the US had failed to properly evaluate whether imports from China were in "such increased quantities" and "increasing rapidly" as stated in Paragraphs 16.1 and 16.4 of the Protocol;
 (ii) the US had statute implementing the causation standard of Paragraph 16 into US law was inconsistent 'as such' with Paragraphs 16.1 and 16.4 of the Protocol;
(iii) the US had failed to properly evaluate whether imports from China were a "significant cause" as stated in Paragraphs 16.1 and 16.4 of the Protocol;
 (iv) the US had imposed a transitional safeguard measure that went beyond the "extent necessary", and that was therefore inconsistent with Paragraph 16.3 of the Protocol; and
 (v)   the US had imposed a transitional safeguard measure for a three-year period that went beyond "such period of time" that was "necessary", and that was therefore inconsistent with Paragraph 16.6 of the Protocol.

Regarding China's claims under GATT 1994, China asked the panel to determine if:

 (i)   the transitional safeguard measure was inconsistent with Article I(1) of the GATT 1994, as the US did not accord the same treatment that it grants to passenger vehicle and light truck tires originating in other countries to like products originating in China; and
 (ii) the transitional safeguard measure was inconsistent with Article II(1b) of the GATT 1994, as the tariffs consist of unjustified modifications of US concessions on passenger vehicle and light truck tires under the GATT 1994.

China asked that the panel recommend that the US promptly comply with its obligations and withdraw the measure. The United States asked the panel to reject China's claims in their entirety.

An Evaluation of the WTO Compatibility of TPSSMs in the Eyes of the WTO Panel

As China's request suggested, whether the TPSSM is compatible with the WTO depends on how the WTO panel perceives the relationship between Paragraphs 16.1 and 16.4 of the Protocol.

China argued that the phrase "in such increased quantities" in Paragraph 16.1 of the Protocol, which also appears in Article 2.1 of the Agreement on Safeguards, was a base level requirement in addressing increasing imports under the Protocol. In accordance with case law under the Agreement on Safeguards, China argued that imports, as a first step, needed to be sudden enough, sharp enough, and significant enough to cause injury. Only after that first step had been achieved would the focus then shift to Paragraph 16.4 of the Protocol where imports would also need to meet the requirement of "increasing rapidly."

The panel rejected this approach, finding that Paragraph 16.4 clarified the substance of the conditions for taking action under paragraph 16 of the Protocol — i.e., that imports had to be "increasing rapidly" and that there had to be "a significant cause" of material injury to the domestic industry. Therefore, in this regard the panel's findings focused on Paragraph 16.4 of the Protocol rather than Paragraph 16.1.

Essentially, China's claims focused on five issues:

(i)   China argued that despite the absolute increases in subject imports, a decline in the rate of increase in the final year of the period of investigation (2008) meant that subject imports were not "increasing rapidly" in accordance with Paragraph 16.4 of the Protocol. The panel disagreed and found that subject imports were increasing rapidly, both absolutely and relatively, in accordance with the Protocol.

(ii)   China asserted that the definition of "contributes significantly" as used by the US in its statute was at odds with the ordinary meaning of the "significant cause" standard in Paragraph 16.4 of the Protocol. The panel rejected this 'as such' argument.

(iii)   China claimed that the USITC failed to properly demonstrate that the imports in question were a "significant cause" of market disruption. China's claim was based on three principal arguments: (1) a failure by the USITC to show conditions of competition between subject imports and the domestic product to support a finding of causation; (2) a failure by the USITC to establish any temporal correlation between rapidly increasing subject imports and material injury to the domestic industry; and (3) a failure by the USITC to address alternative causes of material injury to the domestic industry. The panel rejected all of China's arguments.

(iv)   China claimed that the remedy applied in this case was inconsistent with Paragraph 16.3 of the Protocol as it was not limited to the market disruption caused by rapidly increasing imports. Also, contrary to Paragraph 16.6, the three-year duration exceeded the period of time necessary to prevent or remedy the market disruption. The panel found that China had failed to establish a *prima facie* case in relation to both of these claims regarding the application of these remedies.

(v) The panel found that China's claims under GATT 1994 were dependent on its claims under Paragraph 16 of the Protocol. Therefore, these claims were similarly unsuccessful.

The panel concluded that, in imposing the transitional safeguards measure on 26 September 2009 with respect to imports of tires from China, the US did not fail to comply with its obligations under Paragraph 16 of the Protocol and Articles I(1) and II(1) of the GATT 1994. The panel also found that there was no 'as such' violation regarding the US statute in its implementation of the causation standard of paragraph 16 of the Protocol.

On 27 January 2011, China and the US requested the DSB to adopt a draft decision extending the 60-day time period stipulated in Article 16.4 of the DSU to 24 May 2011. At its meeting on 7 February 2011, the DSB agreed that, upon a request by China and the US, the DSB shall, no later than 24 May 2011, adopt the panel report, unless the DSB decides by consensus not to do so, or either country notifies the DSB of its decision to appeal pursuant to Article 16.4 of the DSU.

VI. Concluding Remarks

The provision of TPSSMs was adopted when China was eager to join the WTO, and the existing WTO members took advantage of this circumstance. Accordingly, TPSSMs are undeniably a set of discriminatory trade measures targeting products from China. It is no exaggeration to say that the provision of TPSSMs is 'China-specific' and therefore contravenes the WTO system's rule of non-discrimination. Although it is understandably unhappy with the use of the mechanism by its trade partners, China will be bound by the TPSSMs provision until it expires. As the case of the US use of TPSSMs indicated, the resentment against the TPSSMs remain a source of tension in trade relations between China and other WTO members.

The WTO panel rejected all of China's claims in the case. The Appellate Body further upheld the panel findings and thus confirmed the legitimacy of the TPSSMs provision in the WTO Protocol.[10] So far, the political and economic damage has been limited because the case only concerned relatively narrow issues. Nevertheless, the conflict between China and the EU over the possible use of European TPSSMs against China may develop into a much more serious challenge to the legitimacy and credibility of the multilateral trade regime.

To ease the tension, the EU should exercise restraint in using the TPSSMs provision against Chinese products. For China, it is apparently not advisable 'to cancel or void' the provision of TPSSMs based solely on the mindset that the provision "was a commitment made under the condition of coerced and limited will".[11] As a rising political and economic power, what China can do is to take positive countermeasures to avoid or reduce the application of and to prevent the abuse of TPSSMs in order to protect its trade interests. That is to say, when a WTO member decides to initiate investigations for TPSSMs, it is more advisable for China to exploit the consultation mechanism to settle trade disputes at their outset and, where necessary, resort to the dispute settlement mechanism of the WTO.

---

[10] http://www.wto.org/english/tratop_e/dispu_e/cases_e/ds399_e.htm (last accessed September 30, 2011).

[11] See footnote 1.

CHAPTER 8

THE CHINESE AND EU APPROACHES TO DISPUTE SETTLEMENT IN THE WTO AND THEIR IMPLICATIONS

The surge in trade disputes between China and the EU in recent years highlight the importance of dispute settlement. Against this backdrop, it goes without saying how important the WTO dispute settlement mechanism is vis-à-vis the settlement of trade disputes. This becomes more prominent when bilateral trade relations between the disputing parties is fragile and tense. Dispute settlement plays an important role when both parties intend to maintain their trade relationship at a certain level. In other words, the function of the dispute settlement mechanism is just to maintain the relationship between the disputing parties.

I. An Overview of the WTO Dispute Settlement Mechanism

The WTO Dispute Settlement System is based on the 'Dispute Settlement Understanding' or simply the 'DSU'. There are essentially four phases in the WTO dispute settlement process: consultations, the panel process, the appellate process and surveillance of implementation.

Phase 1 — Consultations

A WTO member may ask for consultations with another WTO member if the complaining member believes that the other member has violated a WTO agreement, or otherwise nullified or impaired benefits accruing to it. The goal of the consultation stage is to enable the disputing parties to better understand the factual situation and the legal claims with respect to the dispute and to resolve the matter without further proceedings.

The DSU states that "[t]he aim of the dispute settlement mechanism is to secure a positive solution to a dispute. A solution mutually acceptable to the parties to a dispute and consistent with the [WTO] agreements is clearly to be preferred."

Despite the fact that the structure of consultations is undefined, with no rules to guide their conduct, consultations lead to settlements (or at least the apparent abandonment of a case) in around 50% of all cases where a consultation has been requested.

Phase 2 — The Panel Process

If consultations fail to resolve the dispute within 60 days of the request for consultations, the complaining WTO member may request the Dispute Settlement Body (the DSB, which is the WTO organ supervising dispute settlement) to establish a panel to rule on the dispute. The DSB is required to do this, unless there is a consensus in the DSB to the contrary.

The parties to the dispute are supposed to agree on the panelists to form the three-person *ad hoc* panel, which usually comprises current or former government officials. However, in recent cases most appointments have been made by the WTO Director-General.

There are at least two hearings, with written and oral submissions by both parties and questions from the panel, such that the panel is actively engaged in understanding the case.

If a panel finds that a WTO rule has been violated, the standard practice is to recommend that the policy that has been found to be in violation be brought into conformity with WTO rules.

After its circulation to WTO members, the final report is referred to the DSB for formal adoption, which is to take place within 60 days unless there is a consensus not to adopt the report, or an appeal is lodged with the WTO Appellate Body. This so-called negative consensus rule is a fundamental change from the GATT dispute settlement system, where a positive consensus was needed to adopt a panel report, thus permitting a dissatisfied losing party to block any action on the report. Now, as long as one member wants the report adopted, it will be adopted. While the losing party cannot block the adoption of a report, it does have a right of appeal.

Phase 3 — The Appellate Process

The possibility of an appeal to an Appellate Body is a new feature of the WTO dispute settlement system. The Appellate Body consists of seven individuals, appointed by the DSB for four-year terms. An individual may only serve a maximum of two such terms.

The Appellate Body hears appeals of panel reports in groups of any three of its members, although its rules provide for the group hearing a case to exchange views with the other four Appellate Body members before finalizing its report. The Appellate Body is required to issue its report within 90 (but normally 60) days from the date of the appeal, and its report is to be adopted automatically by the DSB within 30 days, barring any consensus to the contrary.

There have been 100 Appellate Body reports as of the end of 2010. In 10 cases, the panels were upheld; in 5 cases, they were reversed. In the remaining 77 cases, the Appellate Body modified, sometimes extensively, the panel's findings.[1]

Phase 4 — Surveillance of Implementation

The final phase of the WTO dispute settlement process is the surveillance stage.

This is designed to ensure that DSB recommendations (based on panel/Appellate Body reports that have been adopted) are implemented. As noted above, if a panel finds that an agreement has been violated, it typically recommends that the member concerned ensures that the offending measure is modified or rescinded in order to conform with WTO obligations.

Under the surveillance function, the offending member is required to state its intentions with respect to implementation. If immediate implementation is impractical, the member is to be afforded a reasonable period of time for implementation. In the absence agreement, that period of time may be set by arbitration. As a guideline for the arbitrator, the DSU states that the period should not exceed 15 months, with the average being 8 to 9 months.

If the offending party fails to implement the report within the reasonable period of time, the prevailing party may request compensation. If that is not forthcoming, it may request the DSB to authorize it to suspend concessions (i.e., take retaliatory action) owed to the non-implementing party. DSB authorization is automatic, barring consensus to the contrary,

---

[1] See WTO Appellate Body Annual Report (2010) WT/AB/15, Annex 4, 18 July 2011; and http://www.wto.org/english/tratop_e/dispu_e/dispu_status_e.htm (last accessed September 30, 2011).

with the degree of suspension subject to arbitration if requested by the non-implementing member.

If the losing party takes corrective action, but there is a dispute over whether the new measure is WTO-consistent, then the current practice is to refer the matter to the original panel, which considers the new measure. It is accepted that this panel report may be appealed. At the end of this process, retaliatory action may be authorized.

It is important to note that retaliation is prospective — it starts when authorized — and is limited to offsetting the future trade effects of the contested measure.

II. An Empirical Study of the Strategic Use of the WTO Dispute Settlement Mechanism

Dispute Settlement Proceedings as Procedural Tactics

The shift towards a rule-oriented system of dispute settlement has not only contributed to further stability and predictability of the international trade regime. The effectiveness of the new system has also been taken into account by member states which, for strategic purposes, aim to foster 'larger systemic interests' in the international trade regime.

A tendency for the dispute settlement mechanism to be used strategically had likewise been recognized by the Sutherland Report. In its assessment on the future of the dispute settlement mechanism, the Report states the following, "It is clear that the members find it useful to utilize the new system as a tool for enhancing their diplomacy and securing solid and reasonably timely responses to practical trade problems." In implying a "litigate and negotiate" approach to the WTO, the Report confirms that states consider the automatic nature of the dispute settlement system and its strict timelines for any procedural steps as an incentive to initiate dispute settlement proceedings in order to obtain timely reasonable judicial decisions for their trade problems.

Consequently, in addition to the primary objective of the dispute settlement mechanism, namely, the settlement of bilateral disputes, member states have increasingly utilized the dispute settlement mechanism to improve their bargaining position through negotiating "in the shadow of the law" and clarifying existing WTO obligations (Petersmann, 2005). These strategic uses of the dispute settlement mechanism provide the respective country with a tactic that improves its bargaining position in bilateral or multilateral negotiations. Bargaining "in the shadow of the law" refers to situations in which the mere possibility of dispute settlement proceedings being initiated induces the opponent to negotiate trade concessions or to settle trade disputes at an early stage. In such situations, even without a credible threat of retaliation from a complainant, the political and economic uncertainty that is related to an adverse ruling may serve as an incentive for the defendant to make concessions or to settle disputes early. In short, "it is thus the threat of legal condemnation, rather than a ruling *per se,* that induces settlement."

In contrast to negotiations "in the shadow of the law", the second strategic use aims to institute dispute settlement proceedings in order to achieve a judicial clarification of contested WTO rules.

Dispute Settlement Proceedings as a Surrogate for Negotiation-Based Rule-Making

Having outlined the different forms of possible strategic dispute settlements used by WTO members, it would likewise be interesting to know why countries fall back on the dispute settlement mechanism to promote their interests. Among other explanations such as identifying the need for additional WTO rules, or putting pressure on other members to engage in negotiations, two main reasons for strategic use of the dispute settlement mechanism seem to stand out. Firstly, the WTO legislative process is often incapable of responding to the need for additional rules and clarification of existing WTO obligations, and secondly, WTO decisions often have far-reaching implications.[2]

The first main reason for an increasingly strategic use of the dispute settlement mechanism can be attributed to the "obvious lack of adequate political rule-making mechanisms for clarifying and complementing WTO rules" within the WTO. As a direct consequence of consensus decision making under Article IX of the Agreement Establishing the WTO, legislative processes in the WTO, conducted between 153 WTO member states, progress slowly. They often result in agreements which have been drafted in a vague manner, leaving scope for interpretation, in order to satisfy the

---

[2] Petersmann, E.-U. (2005). Strategic use of WTO dispute settlement proceedings for advancing WTO negotiations on agricultural subsidies. In Ernst-Ulrich Petersmann (ed), *Reforming the World Trading System Legitimacy, Efficiency, and Democratic Governance,* Oxford University Press: Oxford.

interests of all member states. For this reason, existing provisions under WTO Agreements usually need further clarification. Taking into consideration the need for further clarification and the procedural constraints on decision making in the WTO, member states may increasingly resort to the dispute settlement mechanism as an useful alternative to the comparatively lengthy consensus-based rule making process in the WTO.

The necessity of further interpretation of WTO provisions, and the incapability of the decision-making process to address this need, has shifted power from the law-making organs to judicial organs within the WTO and thus conferred certain *de facto* power to panels and the Appellate Body (AB) to "interpret and effectively make WTO law".

In principle, the negotiating history of the DSU does not indicate any intention of the member states, to confer the power of judicial law-making on the AB when agreeing upon the legalization of the dispute settlement. Although the DSU provides for restrictions on judicial law-making under Article 3(2) DSU, the AB has thus far engaged in substantial judicial law-making in order to fill legal gaps and to clarify ambiguities under existing Agreements. The interpretation of the WTO Treaty by the AB has contributed to clarifying existing obligations, which serves as a guide for member states to understand the scope of their own obligations and to define a breach of WTO obligations by other member states. Furthermore, comprehensive jurisprudence of panel and AB decisions has further developed the WTO legal system and directly affects specific economic outcomes of disputes.

Defense of Systemic Interests Through Participation in Dispute Settlement

Due to the far-reaching implications of judicial decisions in the WTO, member states consider participation in the dispute settlement mechanism to be essential for shaping the interpretation and application of WTO law and to influence the 'systemic effects' of WTO jurisprudence on future cases. Therefore, countries generally have an interest in participating in the dispute settlement system in order to defend their 'larger systemic interests' in the WTO.

Participation in the DSU takes either the form of being a party to the dispute or of being an interested third party. If a member state considers its interests or rights to have been violated by another contracting party, this state can initiate proceedings by making a request for consultations under Article 4 DSU or, in a situation where consultations fail, by directly requesting the establishment of a panel under Article 6 DSU. In addition to securing the interests of the complainant, the DSU also foresees the possibility of other members states joining the proceedings either as co-complainants or as third parties. As an interested third party, a member state has the right to be heard by the panel and to make written submissions to it. In addition, third parties receive the submissions of the parties to the dispute. Based on the procedural options provided by the DSU, a state which is not a party to the dispute might nevertheless have an interest to join as a third party in order to preserve its procedural rights and to influence the outcome of the dispute. For this reason, much discretion is left to the states themselves as to whether or not to defend their interests by means of initiating dispute settlement proceedings. Strategically, any state which is not a party to the dispute but nevertheless has an interest in the specific case would be well advised to make use of the opportunity to become a third party. However, even though all WTO members have equal access to the dispute settlement mechanism in principle, evidence suggests a less frequent use of the mechanism by developing countries. This can be taken as an indication that a country is "less likely to participate in WTO litigation, if it has inadequate power for trade retaliation, if it is poor and does not have the capacity to absorb substantial legal costs or if it is particularly reliant on the responding country for bilateral assistance [...]".[3] Despite the asymmetric representation of WTO members in dispute settlement proceedings, participation from developing countries has nevertheless increased under the new WTO dispute settlement procedure, making it more difficult for larger countries to influence developing countries to give up their legal complaint. Therefore, the automatic nature of the mechanism also seems to be a main advantage for developing countries, as its provides them with a tool to take on economically stronger countries and to obtain a judicial decision if they choose to do so.

III. The Chinese Approach to the WTO Dispute Settlement Mechanism

In this regard, one should first examine the Chinese approach to dispute settlement and its practice of settling disputes. One should note that

---

[3] See Bawn, C.P. (2005). Participation in WTO dispute settlement: Complainants, interested parties, and free riders. *The World Bank Economic Review*, 19(2), p. 302.

peaceful settlement of international disputes can appear in the form of both a political solution and a juridical solution in international law. However, the well-established position of China only encompasses the former, which features mediation, conciliation and negotiation. In other words, China has its own understanding of the peaceful settlement of international disputes. Up to now, China has never required or urged the disputing parties to resolve their disputes by juridical means, whether as a third party or as a permanent member of the United Nations Security Council.

China also takes the stand that disputes of any nature among sovereign states should be resolved through dialogue, because it is not only helpful for all disputing parties to have a better understanding of each other, to clarify the facts and resolve contradictions, but it can also avoid bringing tragedies upon the citizens of all disputing states. Dialogue is a proper approach to the peaceful resolution of international disputes.[4] Apparently, the dialogue approach that China advocates is equivalent to consultation and negotiation, which is an important approach to the political settlement of international disputes.

Negotiation, Consultation and Dialogues

Negotiation, consultation and dialogues are the preferred means of international dispute settlement whenever China is a party to the dispute.[5] The Chinese government is investing heavily in senior level government-to-government dialogues in an effort to talk its way out of current trade problems and avoid future disputes.

China has also established new bilateral and regional cooperation mechanisms with a host of foreign governments, including Argentina, Brazil, the European Union, India, and South Korea, to resolve trade disputes promptly. A recent agreement to establish a China-ASEAN

---

[4] Wang, H. (1998). Speech on the Report of the Special Political Committee of the Charter of the United Nations at the 41st Meeting in the Sixth Committee of the United Nations General Assembly. *Chinese Yearbook of International Law* 827.

[5] For example, in the Agreement on Trade and Economic Cooperation between the European Economic Community and the People's Republic of China, the authority solely entrusted with settling the disputes arising from the implementation of the Agreement is a Joint Committee comprising representatives of the European Economic Community on the one hand and representatives of the People's Republic of China on the other.

regional dispute resolution body could help China contain trade disputes within the region.

Negotiations, consultations and dialogues are also always visible in China's practices in international dispute settlement. In China's diplomacy, a lot of issues of vital importance to China, as well as those rooted in history, were settled through direct negotiations and consultations between the Chinese government and governments of other countries concerned.[6] In the past decade, disputes have often arisen between China and the EU concerning trade in textiles and so on, and these have occasionally escalated to such a point that both parties were about to impose retaliatory trade measures against each other. Interestingly, by means of negotiation, an understanding was always reached before an imminent trade war broke out. For instance, despite its hardline tactics and strong rhetoric on textile trade, China negotiated textile restraint agreements with major trade partners in 2005, which included the EU and the US. Similarly, faced with the threat of WTO action, China has backed down from using tax rebate and tariff policies to boost localization of its semiconductor and auto sectors, respectively.[7]

These negotiations, consultations and dialogues allow China time to defuse tensions and, in some instances, delay the implementation of certain measures. In the case of textiles, drawing out talks allowed a higher export baseline — on which quotas are negotiated — to develop.

---

[6] It was through negotiations that China settled other disputes relating to its sovereignty, such as the question of Hong Kong and Macao. After 22 rounds of deliberate and patient negotiation that started in 1983, an agreement was finally reached between the United Kingdom and China on the handover of Hong Kong to China, i.e., the Joint Declaration of the Government of the United Kingdom of Great Britain and Northern Ireland and the Government of the People's Republic of China on the Question of Hong Kong. The successful resolution of the question of Hong Kong by means of negotiation set up a model for the resolution of the question of Macao. In 1985, as the Chinese premier and the premier of Portugal had friendly consultations on the question of Macao, both parties agreed to start negotiation in Beijing in 1986. After four rounds of negotiations from 1986 to 1987, the Joint Declaration of the Government of the People's Republic of China and the Government of the Republic of Portugal on the Question of Macao was reached in Beijing.

[7] (2005). 'Will textile dispute lead to trade war?' *Xinhua News Agency*, June 2. http://www.china.org.cn/english/international/130777.htm, and (2005). 'China, EU reach deal to settle textile dispute', *Xinhua News Agency*, June 11. http://www. china.org.cn/english/2005/Jun/131667.htm (last accessed September 30, 2011).

In manufacturing, lengthy negotiations allow enough time for a domestic industry, such as auto manufacturing or steel, to gain strength before going head to head with global competitors. In services, such as insurance and telecommunications, they allow China to delay licensing firms and hold off on removing burdensome investment requirements. The consolidation of trade issues into periodic dialogues allows China to persuade its trade partners to prioritize problems and deal with them in more systematic and manageable ways. This tactic may also help combat the perception that thousands of market access issues remain unresolved. Following allegations last year — from both domestic media and neighbors such as Japan, South Korea, Taiwan, and Hong Kong — that Chinese beer and seafood contained unsafe additives, and after parasites were discovered in Chinese kimchi on the eve of the Asia-Pacific Economic Cooperation summit in November 2005, Beijing also negotiated a new bilateral forum on food standards with South Korea.

The Practices of China on the Juridical Solution to International Disputes

China has been keen in resolving international disputes by diplomatic means such as negotiation and consultation, but it is quite cautious towards the two juridical means — international arbitration and judicial solution. The reason for this is China's reluctance to be sued in an international forum, be it an international court or through international arbitration. More or less, this reflects that China does not trust the international judicature, or at least that China feels a sense of estrangement.

International arbitration

In the late 1980s, China changed its attitude towards arbitration as a means to international dispute settlement.[8] When it signed, acceded to or ratified international conventions, China began to have no reservations to arbitration provisions included therein. Significantly, these conventions are

---

[8] In all the treaties and agreements — except some foreign trade agreements — that China had signed before the 1980s, there were no arbitration clauses. China made reservations, if permitted, to almost all the arbitration clauses in the multilateral treaties and international conventions that China signed, acceded to or ratified.

concerned with the economy, trade, technology, transportation, aviation, environment, healthcare, and other professional and technical cooperation.[9] Meanwhile, arbitration clauses and dispute settlement clauses in general (including arbitration) were seen in treaties and agreements on bilateral trade, investment, technology cooperation and cultural exchanges. For example, according to Article 6 of the Agreement between the United States of America and the People's Republic of China on Investment Insurance and its accompanying Exchange Notes, if the dispute cannot be resolved through negotiation, the government of either party may submit an application for arbitration. Similar provisions are incorporated in the bilateral investment agreements between China and other countries, such as France, the United Kingdom, the Netherlands and Canada. However, the bilateral treaties on extradition or judicial assistance which China has signed contain no provisions concerning dispute settlement by arbitration, only clauses for dispute settlement by diplomatic methods or negotiation and consultation.[10]

At the same time, the Chinese government began to actively take part in the activities of the Permanent Court of Arbitration (PCA) actively. In 1993, China appointed four arbitrators to the PCA.

---

[9] In 1988, China acceded to the Convention Establishing the Multilateral Investment Guarantee Agency, which requires that the disputes between a contracting state and the organization be settled by means of negotiation, mediation or arbitration. When it ratified the Convention on the Settlement of Investment Disputes between States and Nationals of Other States in 1992, China agreed to submit the disputes between itself and nationals of any other contracting states concerning expropriation and compensation to the ICSID Center. When it ratified the United Nations Convention to Combat Desertification in Those Countries Experiencing Serious Drought and/or Desertification, Particularly in Africa in 1996 and the Convention of the International Telecommunication Union, the International Telecommunication Convention in 1997, China did not make reservations to the arbitration clauses therein.

[10] The Extradition Treaty between the People's Republic of China and the Kingdom of Thailand, Article 19; the Treaty on the Civil and Commercial Legal Assistance between the People's Republic of China and the Kingdom of Spain, Article 28; the Treaty Concerning Judicial Assistance in Criminal Procedures between the People's Republic of China with Canada, Article 32, and other judicial assistance treaties between China and Greece, the Republic of Korea, Singapore and the US respectively have such similar provisions.

Judicial solutions

Based on the principle that all sovereign states are equal and independent, the Chinese government insists that without the consent, no other country or international organization has power to exercise jurisdiction over another sovereign state.[11]

One notes that international conventions that China has acceded to or ratified contained no clauses by which contracting parties shall resolve the disputes between them by referring disputes to the ICJ. If such clauses do exist in those conventions, China makes reservations to the clauses without exception.

Nevertheless, China's attitude towards the settlement of international disputes by the ICJ has undergone a change. China became more open to such provisions when it began to accede to or ratify international conventions. Where conventions are concerned with the economy, trade, aviation, the environment and other professional activities, China tends not to make reservations to such clauses mandating the use of the ICJ and other international adjudicatory bodies by disputing contracting parties.[12] China acceded to the United Nations Convention on the Law of the Sea in 1998. Part XV of the Convention requires that State Parties to the Convention settle any dispute between them concerning the interpretation or application of the Convention by peaceful means in accordance with Article 2, Paragraph 3 of the Charter of the United Nations and shall seek a solution by the means indicated in Article 33, Paragraph 1 of the Charter. However, should a settlement not be reached, Article 286 of the Convention stipulates that the dispute be submitted at the request of any disputing party to a court or tribunal that has jurisdiction in this

---

[11] In 1972, soon after the resumption of its seat in the United Nations, the People's Republic of China announced that the statement, which the former Republic of China made to accept the compulsory jurisdiction of the International Court of Justice (ICJ), ceased to be effective. China has signed no special agreements with other countries that mandate disputes be submitted to the ICJ.

[12] For example: when China signed and ratified the Convention on the Production, Stockpiling and Use of Chemical Weapons and on Their Destruction, it did not make a reservation to Article 14, a dispute settlement provision which provides that disputes be submitted to the ICJ on the condition that all the disputing parties agree to do so.

regard.[13] It is noted that China has so far referred no relevant dispute to the ICJ or the International Tribunal for the Law of the Sea for a solution.

Not long after China's accession to the WTO, China's attitude towards the WTO dispute settlement mechanism was tested. The US imposed safeguard measures against steel imports from China, the EU and other countries. After a few rounds of consultations failed, the EU brought the dispute to the DSB of the WTO. China joined the process. This was the first time that China had resorted to an international institution for a solution to a dispute.

The dispute with the US concerning steel safeguard measures has been one of the few cases that China referred to the DSB. China seems restrained in initiating the dispute settlement proceedings in the WTO. The following might explain China's inaction:

(i)   Uncertain outcome of the WTO dispute settlement procedure. Although previous WTO rulings, such as the hormone beef case, suggest that the outcome of a dispute settlement procedure is likely to support the Chinese position on the regulation of trade, factors such as the political sensitivity of the case, the potential damage in terms of legitimacy which a positive ruling could inflict on the WTO, and different interpretations of WTO rules, might have induced the WTO to depart from its previous approach.

(ii) Precedent function of negative WTO ruling. In addition to its direct effects on trade in Chinese products, if it were recognized as a precedent, a ruling which did not support the Chinese position might have had repercussions on future similar trade disputes.

(iii) Impact on WTO credibility. A negative ruling might also reduce the credibility of the WTO as an organization promoting trade liberalization.

---

[13] Article 287 of the Convention defines those courts or tribunals as:

(a) The International Tribunal for the Law of the Sea (established in accordance with Annex VI of the Convention) including the Seabed Disputes Chamber;

(b) The International Court of Justice;

(c) An arbitration tribunal constituted in accordance with Annex VII of the Convention; and

(d) A special arbitration tribunal constituted in accordance with Annex VIII for one or more of the categories of disputes specified therein.

(iv) Enforcement problems. A successful WTO challenge, and even the imposition of severe trade sanctions, does not always bring about a change in the position of the offending party. Given the high degree of politicization of the EU policy of imposing special safeguard measures against China, this may also apply to the trade dispute over the European SSG regulations.

However, it is intriguing to note that China has been even more withdrawn when it is brought to the DSB. In two other cases, China was brought before the DSB in 2004 for its policy on tax rebates for integrated circuits exports and in 2006 for duties on auto parts imports. In the semiconductor case, when China received the notification that the US had requested the DSB to establish a panel, it was unhappy because it had not been given adequate opportunity for consultation.[14] As a matter of fact, upon China's insistence, the two parties reached a solution even prior to the initiation of the panel process.

IV. The EU's Approach to the WTO Dispute Settlement Mechanism

The EU is active in promoting its perceived interests in all ways, including by using its trade defense instruments. This may lead to disputes with its major trade partners.

On the other hand, the EU is one of the key players in the WTO. It has not only played a major role in the shaping of the GATT/WTO. In fact, the results of the Uruguay Round negotiations clearly put a much more judicial-oriented dispute settlement system in place. That occurred largely because the EU decided that a more adjudicative system would be desirable as a means of limiting the US tendency to take unilateral trade action.[15]

---

[14] According to Sun Zhenyu, China's permanent representative to the WTO, the US side filed the complaint while the two sides were still in talks. China expressed regret that it could not understand this decision made by the US. (2004). 'U.S. launches WTO complaint against China', *China Daily*, March 19.

[15] Their hope was that by strengthening the WTO/GATT system through making it more adjudicative and automatic, the US would be less able to complain about the system's inadequacies and therefore less likely to act unilaterally. And in return for their agreement to the more adjudicative system, they insisted on provisions designed to prevent unilateralism. Baroncini, E. (1998). The European community

So far, the dispute settlement system has worked well in solving very important disputes and averting 'trade wars'. For this reason, the EU considers that, overall, the system is functioning well and has helped to ensure real market-opening. Moreover, it compares extremely well with other international dispute settlement systems in terms of speed and efficiency. By providing a multilateral forum for settling disputes, the mechanism guards weaker members against unilateral action by the strongest.

The EU is also a frequent user of the WTO dispute settlement mechanism. Trade negotiators from powerful countries see the primary function of the WTO dispute settlement system as helping to enforce the terms of agreements reached through the WTO legislative process. It is even argued that the EU appears to make an excessive use of the dispute settlement mechanism.

As it boasts, however, the EU never initiates dispute settlement proceedings before exhausting all other ways of solutions.[16]

V. Concluding Remarks

China's accession to the WTO evidenced the nation's commitment to subject itself to the jurisdiction of international dispute settlement mechanisms, which are similar to traditional judicial means. This signifies that the Chinese practice of settling international disputes has undergone a significant change.

The WTO regime governs the settlement of disputes between China and the EU. The rule-based dispute settlement mechanism aims to provide predictability in trade relations among WTO members. However, this does not change China's strong preference for political solutions (especially through means of consultation and negotiation which rule out the possibility of any third party involvement).

---

and the diplomatic phase of the WTO dispute settlement understanding. In P. Eeckhout and T. Tridimas (eds), *Yearbook of European Law*, Volume 18. Oxford University Press: New York.

[16] http://ec.europa.eu/trade/tackling-unfair-trade/dispute-settlement/(last accessed September 30, 2011).

CHAPTER 9

TRADE DISPUTES BETWEEN CHINA AND THE EU: ARE THEY MANAGEABLE?

I. Introduction

For the foreseeable future, trade disputes between China and the EU cannot be avoided, and the WTO dispute settlement mechanism will remain a main channel for the management of such disputes. Now the issue is the level of effectiveness with which disputes between China and the EU can be managed in the WTO.

II. China-EU Trade Disputes: Misplaced or Manageable in the WTO?

Approach to Trade Disputes: China and the EU

That said, international trade disputes are not necessarily incurable blights to international trade relations between disputing nations. The answer to the question of whether trade disputes between China and the EU can be managed depends on their respective approaches to such disputes. This section will look into the respective approaches of both China and the EU towards trade disputes.

China's approach to trade disputes

As a party to international disputes concerning territorial integrity, sovereignty and other vital interests of the nation, China has often been seen to be hostile to any judicial solution and to have demonstrated a strong preference for political solutions (especially through means of consultation and negotiation which rule out the possibility of any third-party involvement). With the increasing integration of the country into the

127

international community due to globalization, China can now afford to follow a less stringent attitude towards other disputants and pursue a more balanced policy towards the rest of the world. Accordingly, China has accepted more and more juridical solutions, especially international arbitration, as the means to the settlement of international disputes.

Needless to say, China's approach to trade disputes cannot be more evidently exhibited than in its approach to the WTO dispute settlement mechanism. The WTO established a powerful dispute settlement mechanism to monitor members' regulation of international trade, the aim of which is to provide the multilateral trading system with safety and predictability. This mechanism is governed by the Rules and Procedures on Dispute Settlement Understanding (hereinafter referred to as the Understanding), which is itself an integral part of a package agreement of the WTO. The protection offered by the systematic and normative provisions of the Understanding far exceeds that which is embodied in the General Agreement on Tariffs and Trade (GATT). Institutionally, the WTO dispute settlement mechanism is based upon an international organization which has an international juridical composition and outlook. Moreover, it has a new body called the Dispute Settlement Body (DSB), which is an alter ego. The procedure known as 'negative consensus' is the most prominent feature of the dispute settlement mechanism of the WTO. According to the 'negative consensus' principle, if any party to a trade dispute requests for a panel to resolve the dispute, the panel is to be set up automatically. Unless at least one party to the dispute appeals to the AB, the panel report will come into effect. In case of appeal, the AB will evaluate the legal matters which relate to the panel report.[1] Once the report of the AB is made available, the DSB shall adopt it with the 'negative consensus' principle, and then the AB report comes into effect. The DSB is also responsible for the proper implementation of its 'recommendations'.[2] The party whose trade measures have been found to be in violation with WTO rules should modify or repeal the measures concerned. If the party fails to implement the 'recommendations', which form part of the adopted report, compensation may be imposed on the party or the concessions that the other parties made under the WTO agreement may be withdrawn.[3] Therefore, as far as trade disputes among WTO members are concerned, the dispute settlement mechanism of the WTO is the equivalent of an international court.

---

[1] DSU, Article 17, Paragraph 6.
[2] DSU, Article 21.
[3] DSU, Article 22.

By acceding to this global trade system, China has accepted the jurisdiction of the dispute settlement mechanism of the WTO. This shows that China's approach to the settlement of trade disputes has undergone a significant change. Not long after China's accession to the WTO, China's attitude towards the WTO dispute settlement mechanism was tested. Since its accession to the WTO, China has been brought to the WTO eleven times.[4] It no longer views the use of the WTO dispute settlement mechanism as a hostile act, and instead sees lengthy negotiations as the normal means by which mature trading partners resolve their differences. Moreover, China is learning to use the WTO dispute settlement mechanism, particularly through third-party involvement in disputes, and has become comfortable in using the mechanism.[5]

As of 31 December 2010, there were 21 complaints against China in the WTO, 4 of which were filed in 2010 and still in the consultation stage.[6] It is interesting to find that in most cases that have already been closed, early settlement was reached through China quickly conceding to demands from its trade partners and agreeing to withdraw or modify its WTO-inconsistent measures in less than a year.[7]

In the other five closed cases that were not settled early, China appealed against four panel reports. The percentage of panel reports appealed against is 80%, which is higher than the average appeal rate in the WTO Dispute Settlement Mechanism (68%).[8] It seems that China continued to contest these cases to the end either to win more time to

---

[4] WT/TPR/S/161, 28 February 2006 and WT/TPR/S/199, 16 April 2008.

[5] An indication of China's serious commitment to the WTO has been its assiduous tracking of dispute settlements. Since its accession, it has been a third party to 62 cases, in addition to being a complainant in 3 cases (US Steel Safeguards, US Anti-Dumping and Countervailing Duties on Coated Paper and US Special Safeguards on Wheels) and a respondent in 11 cases.

[6] DS407: China-Provisional Anti-Dumping Duties on Certain Iron and Steel Fasteners from the European Union field by EU; DS413: China-Certain Measures Affecting Electronic Payment Services initiated by the US; DS414: China-Countervailing and Anti-Dumping Duties on Grain Oriented Flat-rolled Electrical Steel from the United States filed by the US; DS419: China-Measures concerning wind power equipment filed by the US.

[7] For example, DS309: China — Value-Added Tax on Integrated Circuits; DS340: China — Measures Affecting Imports of Automobile Parts.

[8] This percentage appealed is limited to the panel reports other than Article 21.5 reports; see WT/AB/13, *Appellate Body Annual Report for 2009*, February 2010, p. 59.

adjust its domestic industry policies and regulations[9] or to be satisfied with having the opportunity to articulate its own interpretation of the often vague WTO provisions.

In conclusion, unlike uncertain, less formal cooperation, the WTO rules of dispute settlement provide the only predictability or stability to a potential investment or trade-development situation. China's WTO accession marks a brand new approach of China to international dispute settlement.

EU's approach to trade disputes

The EU leads in taking measures to promote its presumed interests or the welfare of its citizens. It is very decisive in using trade defense instruments to defend its conceived interests. Both practices may give rise to trade disputes with its major trade partners.[10]

On the other hand, the EU is a common player in dispute resolutions in the WTO. Trade negotiators from powerful countries see the primary function of the WTO dispute settlement system as a tool to help enforce the terms of agreements reached through the WTO legislative process. The EU is a frequent user of the WTO dispute settlement mechanism. The latest case took place on 3 March 2008 when the EU formally requested consultations at the WTO over measures that affect the operation of foreign financial information suppliers in China. China has prevented foreign suppliers of financial information services from providing their services directly to their clients.[11]

---

[9] The average period of time between the establishment of a panel and the expiry of the reasonable peried of time is 775 days, or over two years. If we count from the time when consultations are requested, the average period grows to 1,507 days, or over four years. See TN/DS/W/90, *Diagnosis of the Problems Affecting the Dispute Settlement Mechanism, Some Ideas by Mexico,* July 16, 2007.

[10] For example, while trade defense measures account for a very small proportion of measures reported to the Commission (less than 5%), such measures account for 30% of all EU WTO complaints.

[11] Foreign suppliers are now required to operate through an agent under the umbrella of Xinhua itself. Moreover, Xinhua has recently launched a financial information service in direct competition with foreign suppliers. The relevant Chinese measures appear to breach China's GATT commitments on national treatment and market access, which require that foreign companies can operate in China and are not treated less favourably than local ones. It is also contrary to obligations not to cut back on existing rights for companies and to provide regulatory independence, which China committed to ensure at the time of its WTO accession in 2001.

Positive Role of Consultation

In this regard, the role of consultation in the management of trade disputes between China and the EU should be expounded upon. The WTO dispute settlement process involves four main stages in a typical completed case: consultations, panel process, appeal and implementation. At all phases of this process, WTO members in the dispute are encouraged to consult each other in order to settle disputes 'out of court' and the WTO Director-General is available to offer his good offices to mediate or to help achieve reconciliation.[12] An agreement could be reached between parties prior to a WTO ruling. Such agreements are known as an 'early settlement', and according to a study, these yield the most favorable policy outcome for complainants under the WTO.[13]

For China, the consultation process is in line with the Chinese practice of settling disputes and has, as a matter of fact, become a preferable way to manage trade disputes with other trade partners. 9 of the 14 (about 64%) were settled at the consultation stage or at the panel stage through diplomatic channels before a WTO panel had reached any ruling.

Side Effects of Strategic Uses of WTO Dispute Settlement Mechanism

It is noted that in addition to the primary objective of the dispute settlement mechanism to pursue the settlement of bilateral disputes, the rule-oriented system of dispute settlement may help member states realize strategic purposes which aim to foster the "larger systemic interests" in the international trade regime.

Firstly, in implying a "litigate and negotiate" approach to the WTO, the automatic nature of the dispute settlement system and its strict timelines for any procedural steps can serve as an incentive to initiate dispute settlement proceedings in order to obtain timely reasonable judicial decisions for their trade problems.

Secondly, member states have increasingly instrumentalized the dispute settlement mechanism to improve their bargaining position through negotiating "in the shadow of the law". Such a strategic use of the dispute settlement mechanism provides the respective country with a tactic that

---

[12] See Article 5 of the DSU.

[13] See Busch, M. L. and E. Reinhardt (2003). Developing countries and GATT/WTO dispute settlement. *Journal of World Trade*, 37(4), 719–753.

improves its bargaining position in bilateral or multilateral negotiations. Bargaining "in the shadow of the law" refers to negotiation situations in which the mere possibility to initiate dispute settlement proceedings induces the opponent to negotiate trade concessions or to settle trade disputes at an early stage. In such situations, even without credible threat by a complainant to retaliate, the factor of political and economic uncertainty that is related to an adverse ruling may serve as an incentive for the defendant to make concessions or to settle disputes early. In short, "it is thus the threat of legal condemnation, rather than a ruling per se, that induces settlement."

Thirdly, in contrast to the purpose of negotiations in the "shadow of the law", dispute settlement proceedings may be instituted to pursue the clarification of existing WTO obligations, that is, to achieve a judicial clarification of contested WTO rules.

Fourthly, the WTO dispute settlement proceedings can be used as a surrogate for negotiation based rule making. WTO members fall back on the dispute settlement mechanism to promote their interests, by identifying the need for additional WTO rules, putting pressure on other members to engage in negotiations. In addition, there are two main reasons for strategic use of the dispute settlement mechanism: First, the incapability of the WTO legislative process to respond to the need for additional rules and for the clarification of existing WTO obligations and secondly, the far reaching implications of WTO decisions. Taking into consideration the need for further clarification and the procedural constraints for decision making in the WTO, member states may increasingly resort to the dispute settlement mechanism as an useful alternative for the comparatively lengthy consensus-based rule making process in the WTO. The necessity of further interpretation of WTO provisions, and the incapability of the decision-making process to address this need, has shifted power from the law-making organs to judicial organs within the WTO and thus conferred certain "de facto power" to panels and the Appellate Body "(AB) to interpret and effectively make WTO law".

Fifthly, a WTO member may engage in dispute settlement participation in defense of systemic interests. Due to the far-reaching implications of judicial decisions in the WTO, participation in the dispute settlement mechanism has been considered essential by member states for shaping the interpretation and application of WTO law and to influence the "systemic effects" of WTO jurisprudence on future cases. Therefore, countries generally have an interest to participate in the dispute settlement system in order to defend their "larger systemic interests" in the WTO. Participation in the DSU takes either the form of being a party to the dispute or of being an interested third party. If a member state considers its interests or rights being violated by another contracting party, this state can initiate proceedings by making a request for consultations under Article 4 DSU or, in case of their failure, by directly requesting the establishment of a panel under Article 6 DSU. In addition to secure the interests of the complainant, the DSU also foresees the possibility for other members states to join the proceeding either as a co-complainant or as third party. The participation as interested third party in a dispute preserves the member state the right to be heard by the panel and to make written submissions to it. In addition, third parties receive the submissions of the parties to the dispute. Based on the procedural options provided by the DSU, a member, which is not a party to the dispute, might nevertheless have an interest to join as third party in order to preserve its procedural rights and to influence the outcome of the dispute. For this reason, much discretion is left to the states themselves whether or not to defend their interests by means of initiating dispute settlement proceedings. Strategically, any member which is not a party to the dispute but nevertheless has an interest in the specific case, would be well advised to make use of the possibility to become a third party.

All the strategic uses of the WTO dispute settlement mechanism are made possible as a result of a combination of multiple factors, in particular the fact that there is no limitation on the ability of a member to launch complaints against another member through the WTO dispute settlement mechanism. In other words, the very existence of WTO dispute settlement mechanism provides the incentive for a WTO member to bring others to the dispute settlement body. Such strategic uses of the WTO dispute settlement mechanism carry inherent risks, i.e., they poison trade relations between China and the EU, which in turn nurtures trade disputes between the two parties.

III. Broader Context of Trade Disputes and their Implications

There is a possibility of trade disputes between China and the EU being mismanaged in a broader context, where the legal mechanism is of little assistance. China-EU trade relations are an intricate phenomenon, and changes in the nature of China-EU trade relations mirror the political and economic relationship between the two parties.

In this regard, it might be helpful to bear this in mind: given that the two economies are deeply interconnected and interdependent within global production networks, the deficit is largely a structural one driven by the process of global production sharing. The widely held view that China's rapid penetration of the European market is driven by unfair trade practices needs to be reexamined. To deflect domestic political pressure, EU policy makers could perhaps publicly declare that the 'China deficit' will not be fully addressed until industrial adjustment and productivity growth in the EU are in place,[14] and that expanding trade between the EU and China serves European interests, even when China has a bilateral surplus.

Due in part to this, the EU and China launched the High Level Economic and Trade Mechanism (HLM) in Beijing in April 2008. As mentioned in chapter 4, the HLM, which institutionalized the dialogue between the EC and the State Council of China, at Vice-Premier level, is designed to deal with issues of strategic importance to EU-China trade relations, investment and economic cooperation. For example, HLMs can become the perfect venue for resolving some of the disputed issues in the WTO. The consultation phase of the dispute settlement process will be fully utilised and thus ease the stress of a trade dispute.

The trade defense instruments of the EU are inclined to defend European industries. Anti-dumping and safeguard measures may relieve some of the strains of Chinese competition on the European market. However, it is the EU's and its member states' own reforms such as industrial restructuring that will safeguard their competitiveness in the long run. Criticism of China's trade policies should focus on market access barriers, and unwanted barriers as well as China's trade balance with the world, not China's bilateral surplus with the EU. Therefore, smooth China-EU trade relations will first hinge on how the EU perceives prospective trade disputes between China and the EU and how it minimizes its dependence on trade defense instruments.

More importantly, the EU's obsession with its unique values, particularly human rights and environmental issues, is likely to be a stumbling block to any agenda that is designed to bring the two parties closer. From the EU's perspective, human rights and environmental issues are among the main obstacles preventing closer relations with China. The official EU-China Dialogue on Human Rights works well technically and leads to better mutual understanding, the freeing of dissidents or the signing of the UN conventions on human rights. However, a growing frustration is being felt in Europe because the overall human rights situation in China is not

---

[14] Hoogmartens, J. (2004). *EC Trade Law Following China's Accession to the WTO.* Kluwer Law International: The Hague, pp. 177–178.

showing much progress, or at least not the kind of progress that Europeans would like to see. Growing public pressure might drive the EC to confront China in various ways, for example, by supporting draft resolutions on China in the UN Human Rights Commission.[15] In this case, neither the rhetoric of the China-EU strategic partnership nor the HLM will be able to facilitate a dispute resolution.

As for environmental issues, the highlight is greenhouse gas emissions. China is the second largest emitter after the US. In September 2005, after its unilateral promise to cut carbon dioxide emissions by 40% by 2030, the EU began to press China to commit to a binding scheme, which China has been reluctant to accept, on grounds that this would inhibit its development. As greenhouse gas emissions pose a danger to all mankind, this issue will continue to loom larger and larger in EU-China relations.

IV. Concluding Remarks

From a purely legalistic point of view, the trade disputes between China and the EU can be managed, due to the availability of the WTO dispute settlement mechanism and both parties' willingness to use the legal channels, and perhaps more importantly, due to China's gradual adeptness at using the WTO dispute settlement mechanism.

Ironically, while both China and the EU are increasingly resorting to the WTO dispute settlement mechanism, the excessive use of the DSM can in itself spark disputes. An empirical study on the use of the dispute settlement by India and Brazil as well as by the US and the EU shows how the WTO DSM can be strategically used to successfully defend the 'larger systemic interests' of member states. All these states have been actively engaged in the Doha negotiations and were frequent users of the DSM in the recent past. They do not face the general difficulties of many developing countries when utilising the DSM. While the EU handsomely uses the DSM to defend its larger systemic interests, while China is getting used to such usage of the DSM, this may also lead to conflict between the two

---

[15] The annual meeting of the UN Human Rights Commission has since early 1990s been used by the US and a few international NGOs as a venue to confront China on human rights record. The EU has been occasionally seen to join the call for human rights reform. See Potter, P. (2002). Human rights — social welfare and social control. In Pitman Potter (ed), *The Chinese Legal System-Globalization and Local Culture*. Routledge Curzon: London, pp. 91–92.

parties, since their interests do not often converge. Therefore, whether disputes may arise between the EU and China in relation to the use of the DSM will hinge on an assessment of their participation in the DSM and their expectations behind such a legal approach.

Similarly, the WTO Trade Policy Review Mechanism (TPRM), which is an exercise mandated in the WTO agreements, in which member countries' trade and related policies are examined and evaluated at regular intervals, provides a forum for both China and EU to better understand each other about their respective trade policies, from a legalistic point of view. However, use of the TPRM often goes beyond the designs of the mechanism. The EU uses the review to press China on issues of non-compliance such as government interference, transparency, standards, intellectual property rights protection and discrimination against EU firms China has also taken advantage of the TPRM to challenge the EU in relation to those EC trade measures which have been perceived as unfair. Such use, albeit justified, does not help to resolve existing trade disputes between China and the EU.

Again, it is observed that the EU has been active in applying the biased provisions available in the Protocol on the Accession of China (to the WTO) to deal with its trade concerns with China.[16] From a purely legalistic point of view, the EU is justified in doing so. However, only when the EU refrains from exercising its rights can the possibility of trade disputes be minimized. Of course, the EU can apply trade defense instruments that are justified under the WTO Agreements. In industries where Chinese imports are rising rapidly and genuinely affecting domestic EU firms, the EU may apply the time-limited defense mechanism. Technically speaking, for the sake of avoiding direct confrontation with China, the WTO Safeguard Agreement is preferable to Article 16 of the Protocol on the Accession of China (which allows for product-specific safeguard measures against China). In other words, the EU should shift to normal safeguard measures ahead of the 2013 expiry year of Article 16. To reduce prospective disputes between the EU and China, the granting of market economy status to China is advisable. This would mean that ahead of the 2016 expiry year of Article 15 of the Protocol on the Accession of China (which allows WTO members to designate China as a

---

[16] Chinese observers are often critical of these provisions in the Protocol. Two such examples are Article 15, allows other WTO members to treat China as a non-market economy in determining the existence of dumping and subsidizing, and Article 16, that allows for product-specific safeguard measures against China, etc.

non-market economy in determining price compatibility in antidumping or countervailing investigations), the EU should phase out discrimination against imports from China.

For the EU, the real question in the foreseeable future would be how to help China open its economy and market to more imports and investments in sectors that it still considers as strategic ones and to provide more incentives for China to protect intellectual property rights. Therefore, smooth and healthy China-EU trade relations will hinge on the EU's patience and skills in dealing with a rising China. In the long run, however, maintaining sustainable and healthy China-EU trade relations will depend on how the EU further works to assist in integrating China into the international community. China is now sticking to its vision of a harmonious world and is committed to a peaceful rise. This will provide impetus for the country to look for amicable solutions to trade disputes with the EU.

CHAPTER 10

MANAGEMENT OF CHINA-EU TRADE DISPUTES: BEYOND DISPUTES AND TRADE

I. Introduction

The European Commission goes so far as to say that "China is the single most important challenge for EU trade policy".[1] In its trade relations with the EU,[2] China is pursuing the following: recognition of its market-economy status (MES), stronger disciplines on EU anti-dumping and safeguard measures, removal of peak tariffs on garments, leather goods and other manufactured exports; reduction of agricultural subsidies and tariffs to open markets for its expanding agricultural exports, and less trade-restrictive EU SPS and TBT measures. All these measures restrict China's exports of labor-intensive goods. China has been constantly exercising pressure on the EU to reduce or remove many of these barriers, which would expose inefficient EU producers to even greater Chinese competition.

What do EU exporters and investors expect from the EU's trade relationships with China? The following are some probable aims: a comprehensive tariff cut from a nominal average of 9%, delivery of GATS-plus commitments on services liberalization; removal of foreign-ownership restrictions and better legal protection for EU investors, strengthened disciplines and transparency on all manner of domestic regulation (e.g., on administering subsidies, licenses, safety standards, IPR and customs

---

[1] Quoted from the Europe Commission's Trade website: http://ec.europa.eu/trade/creating-opportunities/bilateral-relations/countries/china/ (last accessed September 30, 2011).

[2] European Commission (2006). *Competition and Partnership: A Policy for EU-China Trade and Investment,* October 24. http://trade.ec.europa.eu/doclib/docs/2006/october/tradoc_130793.pdf (last accessed September 30, 2011).

procedures), binding commitments on government procurement, competition rules and trade facilitation, and commitments on core labor and environmental standards.

On the Chinese side, as things stand China is unlikely to make most of these concessions, just as the EU is unlikely to concede anything major to China. In view of this, trade disputes are inevitable in the high-pressure bilateral trade relations.

On the other hand, as the roles of China and the EU both grow in a globalizing world and both sides see value in deeper relations, they also have doubts about how far and how fast those relations should change under the threat of rising trade disputes. This chapter will first identify the variables affecting China-EU relations in light of trade dispute management. Next, it will argue for an international institutional cooperation between China and the EU to facilitate the management of trade disputes. In the end it will propose a grand strategy design in the light of trade dispute settlement.

II. Variables Affecting China-EU Relations in Light of Trade Dispute Management

Among all aspects of China-EU relations, trade has seen the fastest expansion, going through an intense period of dramatically deepening interactions characterized by expanded cooperation and contacts across the spectrum of public and private engagement. Management of trade disputes and promotion of smooth trade relations should be sought in the broader context of bilateral relations between China and the EU. What variables are then likely to shape China-EU relations? This section identifies five variables that can potentially alter/affect recent progress in China-EU relations.

The first is the impact of trade on the European economies. With the economic rise of China and an expanding EU trade deficit with China, European economies are increasingly feeling the 'China factor'. Thus far, this has not permeated politics in the same way that it has in the US, but voices of concern that advocate protectionism can be heard across the continent. While trade imbalance is justifiable in economic theory, China needs to act to address this issue. After more than twenty years of trade liberalization, China has established a trade regime and formulated a set of laws and regulations that basically conform to the WTO rules and reflect the domestic economic situation, but there is still much to improve upon. At present, China should improve its rules on tax refunds, review its foreign exchange regulation system so as to reduce the economic dependency ratio on foreign trade, change its economic growth strategy from an export-oriented one to a more comprehensive one, strengthen regulation on the export of enterprises, and improve the quality of economic growth.

The second variable is China's degree of responsiveness to numerous issues of concern. China used to be unhappy with outside criticism and demands, but due to its increasingly interdependent relations with the EU, such criticism should be regarded as serious requests put forward by the European side in the spirit of partnership, to advance the China-Europe relationship. China has its requests too — notably lifting the arms embargo and granting of market economy status — that the EU needs to take seriously and be responsive to.

The third variable concerns a clearer definition and milder understanding of the strategic partnership. The strategic partnership definition presents a rosy roadmap for the China-EU relationship, but the underlying discontent arising from the differences between high expectations and harsh reality also adds momentum to trade disputes. Indeed, in the eyes of civil society, various experts on China, as well as NGOs in several EU member states, the strategic partnership is no more than the European Commission's ambitious and optimistic view of China if it is not limited to rosy rhetoric. A realistic China should have a clearer understanding of the bilateral relationship. It should increasingly perceive issues from the perspective of the European Parliament, which represents the wishes of the people of Europe.

A fourth factor that will shape bilateral relations between China and the EU would be the adjustment of European expectations of the pace and scope of internal reforms in China. Although the EU has invested heavily — politically, financially, and rhetorically — in assisting China in a wide range of reforms, it should understand that its influence in China's domestic affairs is rather limited. The EU has viewed China primarily as a developing country and transitional nation in the midst of multiple reforms aimed at liberalizing its economy, globalizing its society, and pluralizing its polity.

Lastly, Europe now expects China to contribute more to global governance. This is made clear in the 2006 Communication and other China-related documents. China may not yet be a global power, but it is increasingly a global actor. As such, Europe (and other nations) will be looking to Beijing to deliver more international public goods and to help address many of the challenges and crises that afflict the international order.

III. International Institutional Cooperation to Facilitate Management of Trade Disputes

Although international cooperation is possible in the view of neo-realists, it is "hard to achieve, difficult to maintain".[3] This is so because, as Waltz claims, "states concern of relative gains than absolute gains", which limits the willingness of states to cooperate.[4] The trade disputes between China and the EU would be a good example of the 'relative gains problem'. When it came to its trade relation with China, the EU wanted a greater 'market share' in mercantile China, and therefore established a series of policies towards China to promote trade between both sides. However, at the same time, the EU also fears that China may achieve relatively greater gains from their cooperation, and therefore surpass the EU as a result. The EU also views an increasingly powerful China as a potentially more dangerous rival. With the fear that 'today's friend may become tomorrow's enemy' in mind, the EU has set up instruments to restrict the competitive challenge from China. For example, the EU has not only relentlessly resorted to its trade defense instruments, but has also shown keen interest in coercing or inducing China to adopt 'voluntary' export restraints. The agreement on clothing and textiles in 2006 is one such example. Naturally, China has adopted corresponding measures as a response. To a certain extent, continued trade disputes prove the assumption that when states always consider their relative gains, international cooperation is hard to maintain.

In this context, in order for trade disputes to be manageable, there needs to be facilitating arrangements between China and the EU that discuss more than just disputes or even trade. Minimally, there should be legal and institutional arrangements. Needless to say, the current bilateral agreements and the WTO agreements serve this purpose.

The legal basis for bilateral trade relations has been the Trade and Cooperation Agreement of 1985. Since then, there have been 7 formal agreements and 22 sectoral and regulatory dialogues on a wide range of issues. On the institutional front, the China-EU Joint Economic and Trade Committee was established in 1985 through the Trade and Economic Cooperation Agreement, in order to promote trade and economic cooperation. The Joint

---

[3] Baylis, J. and S. Smith (2001). *The Globalization of World Politics: An Introduction to International Relations,* 2nd Edition. Oxford University Press: Oxford, p. 190.

[4] Burchill, S. and A. Linklater, eds. (2001). *Theories of International Relations.* 2nd Edition. Houndmills: Palgrave. Chapter 3.

Committee meets annually, with the venue alternating between China and the EU. The meeting is chaired at ministerial level.

China and the EU agreed to a 'strategic partnership' in 2003. In 2007, both sides agreed to start negotiations on a new Partnership and Cooperation Agreement (PCA), which would update and expand bilateral cooperation that has been growing since 1985. The EU intends for the PCA to cover political and economic issues, including its non-trade objectives on democracy, human rights, the rule of law, sustainable development, climate change, and labor and environmental standards. Its trade-and-investment priorities for the PCA include the better enforcement of IPRs, mutual recognition of geographical indicators, WTO-plus commitments on services and investment, lower non-tariff barriers and subsidies, more transparent and open government procurement, improved norms and standards, and better functioning of the legal regime.[5]

The High Level Economic and Trade Mechanism was launched in Beijing in April 2008. The Mechanism is designed to deal with issues of strategic importance of in EU-China trade relations, investment and economic cooperation by strengthening dialogue between the European Commission and the State Council of China at Vice-Premier level. This Mechanism will provide a new tool to address issues of mutual concern, especially in the areas of investment, market access and intellectual property rights protection, as well as other strategic issues related to trade.

Being aware of China's rise and its implications, the EU was and still is a strong supporter of China's integration into the world. This is characterized by the multilateral institutional frameworks that have been established between both parties. For example, in the case of China's accession to the WTO, the EU argued that a WTO without China was not truly universal in scope. For China, the open-door policy symbolized an important step of its integration into the global economic order, and its formal accession to the WTO in December 2001 was the most important move in this direction. The implications of China's commitments in the context of accession to the WTO went far beyond securing improved access for EU firms to China's market, but represented a China willing to accept the existing international legal order and embrace international norms.

However, at the same time that increased institutional cooperation is taking place, pressure is ironically mounting on both China and the EU to

---

[5] European Commission (2006), *op. cit.*

head in a more confrontational direction. For example, the 'high level trade talks' between China and the EU in April 2008 achieved little, despite the fact that the EU sent its largest joint mission to a foreign country for a single meeting in its 50 years of existence. It has been observed that the legal and institutional arrangements seem to be unable to inhibit built-in EU protectionism against China and Chinese foot-dragging on reforms. Hence, it is imperative to bolster the institutional framework for bilateral economic relations — to go beyond low-key, low-level, inconclusive institutional dialogues, which can be successful only if both trading partners are ready to make choices. This will require both China and the EU to rethink their strategies.[6]

This chapter argues that existing international legal frameworks cannot fully address the pressure that arises from the volatile relationship between an aggressive and mercantile China and an impatient EU that seeks to tame it. It further suggests that while institutionalizing a new facilitative legal framework, a second tier arrangement to address trade disputes should be conciliatory trade strategies that fully take into account the fact that each trading partner is the other's largest source of imports.

IV. A Grand Strategy for China-EU Relations in the Light of Trade Dispute Management

From 'Small Bargain' to a 'Grand Bargain'[7]

After a few years of acrimonious complaints against each other, there is a need to reassess existing trade strategies and even re-launch serious negotiations. Renewed assessment and interaction would solely encourage both parties to enforce their WTO commitments better, and shall not be designed for both sides to find faults with each other, let alone secure a

---

[6] Evenett, S. J. (2007). The Trade Strategy of the European Union: Time for a Rethink. University of St. Gallen, Department of Economics Working Paper. http://www.evenett.com/research/workingpapers/BruegelPaper.pdf (last accessed September 30, 2011).

[7] The author acknowledges the following report as his inspiration in formulating this strategy: Messerlin, P. and J. Wang (2008). *Redesigning the European Union's Trade Policy Strategy Towards China.* http://www.ecipe.org/publications/ecipe-working-papers/redesigning-the-european-union2019s-trade-policy-strategy-towards-china/PDF (last accessed September 30, 2011).

WTO-plus commitment. Because it is the richer and larger trading partner, the EU should take the initiative and offer to grant market economy status to Chinese companies in anti-dumping investigations. This move would eliminate the most outrageous biases against Chinese companies in EU anti-dumping procedures, although it may cut EU anti-dumping duties from an average of 40% to roughly 20%.

The EU could reasonably argue that this offer improves its WTO commitments with respect to China. Hence, it could request a similar move from China in the form of a clarification (customs procedures) and/or a better enforcement of China's tariffs (such as on auto parts) to be included in its WTO Protocol Accession.

The small bargain would include no new concessions (which may be left to WTO negotiations). But it would eliminate, reduce, or prevent present and future trade conflicts. As it would also be a public recognition by the EU of China's amazing process of liberalization, which has driven its tariffs close to the EU level, it would restore a climate that would more easily lead to positive and substantive negotiations.

The small bargain should open the door to much more important negotiations on 'behind-the-border' issues. Here, the first task for the EU would be to cut down its endless list of requests by adopting a crucial rule: to push only for those EU export interests that bring clear benefits to Chinese consumers. This rule is economically sound, and it makes a lot of political sense since the Chinese economy is now too big to be successfully influenced by pressure from the outside.

This rule eliminates intellectual property rights (IPRs) as a core topic for negotiations because IPRs tend to increase prices in the importing country without bringing clearly tangible benefits to its consumers. Only the few IPRs — if any — from which Chinese consumers would clearly benefit should be part of the EU's bilateral agenda on IPRs. The other cases should be left to private negotiations and dispute settlements (better IPR enforcement in China will essentially be driven by Chinese forces).

In contrast, the above rule prioritizes negotiations on services, particularly foreign direct investment (FDI) in services where the two trading partners, especially China, have high barriers. What should the EU concede if it wants to get substantial concessions from China on inward FDI in services? Of course, the EU should be ready to offer more market access in services. But such an offer would be of limited interest to China, because not many Chinese service providers would benefit from such an opening in the short- or medium-term. The EU might also offer to renounce, in an early and progressive way, the use of the special safeguard included in Section 16 of China's WTO Accession Protocol. This offer has a clear value in the narrow context of EU-China bilateral trade. But it is also critical in the broader context of the international trade regime, as this special safeguard breaches key WTO principles.

The grand bargain could also include norms as a topic of common interest for both parties. The EU is concerned over the norms ruling China's sovereign wealth funds, while China is concerned over EU norms and standards on imported products. Both cases raise the same key problem: the use of non-trade related regulations in a truly non-discriminatory way.

From Trade Policy to Foreign Policies

China-EU trade disputes are an intricately social phenomenon, and changes in the nature of China-EU trade relations are determined by changes in the political and economic environment. An ambitious trade policy towards China would also have broader international consequences. China's huge potential raises a problem not faced since the late 19th century — how to influence the evolution of an emerging giant in a way that is positive for the multilateral trade regime. Aligning with the US position, which has been the Commission's strategy since early 2007, is not useful for the EU (nor for the US), and it is counterproductive to the extent that it almost inevitably reinforces the arguments of the protectionist camp in Beijing.[8]

Since China's key problem is building the domestic institutions required for sustaining a market economy, the EU should share its experiences in establishing the institutions required by a well-functioning market economy. For China, importing such knowledge may be more politically acceptable than establishing these institutions on its own.

From Rhetoric Strategic Partnership to Genuine Affinity

As David Gosset, founder of the Euro-China Forum, romantically yet insightfully observed, it is precisely based on their affinities that the EU and China have to build a partnership that goes beyond ever-varying trade, scientific or

---

[8] *Ibid.*

even political interests.[9] In other words, by using culture as the keystone of their relationship, the two Eurasian civilizations would be able to enter into a really stable and meaningful cooperation which will have a constructive global impact in the long run.

At the two edges of the Eurasian continent, the EU, a model for cooperation among countries, and China, a reference for developing countries, have a greater role to play in this highly critical global situation.

However, one should not forget that managing the growing interdependence between a post-nation-state Europe and a re-emerging Chinese nation is a process that does presuppose time. An agenda uniquely driven by trade or immediate technocratic concerns does not fully express the nature of the Chinese and European cultures.

China-EU trade relations were largely secondary during the first period of general China-EU relations and gradually came to take centre stage in the third period. At this stage, it should be borne in mind that only a shared awareness of fundamental cultural and historical commonalities can lead to the deepening of the links between the two edges of Eurasia. Better understanding between the EU and China is also necessary for both sides to take full measure of what the two ancient civilizations can achieve together.

V. Concluding Remarks

In conclusion, both China and the EU will need to lower their expectations somewhat, clarify their rosy rhetoric, learn how to live with, narrow, or manage their differences, and develop the mechanisms that are required to build a truly sustainable long-term relationship. Rising trade disputes are still to be expected, but the strong bonds and mutual interests will drive China and the EU closer and closer together over time.

---

[9] Gosset, D. Founder of the *Euro-China Forum*, http://www.ceibs.edu/ase/Documents/8theu_info1.htm (last accessed September 30, 2011).

AGREEMENT ON TRADE AND ECONOMIC COOPERATION BETWEEN THE EUROPEAN ECONOMIC COMMUNITY AND THE PEOPLE'S REPUBLIC OF CHINA — 1985

THE COUNCIL OF THE EUROPEAN COMMUNITIES,

THE GOVERNMENT OF THE PEOPLE'S REPUBLIC OF CHINA,

NOTING with satisfaction the development of friendly relations between the European Economic Community and the People's Republic of China,

CONSIDERING that the Trade Agreement between the European Economic Community and the People's Republic of China, signed on 3 April 1978, has been satisfactorily applied,

INSPIRED by their common will to introduce a new stage into their commercial and economic relations,

DESIRING on the basis of equality and mutual advantage, to intensify and diversify their trade and actively develop economic and technical cooperation in line with their mutual interests,

HAVE DECIDED TO CONCLUDE THIS AGREEMENT, THE TERMS OF WHICH ARE AS FOLLOWS:

Article 1

The two Contracting Parties will endeavour, within the framework of their respective existing laws and regulations, and in accordance with the principles of equality and mutual advantage:

— to promote and intensify trade between them;
— to encourage the steady expansion of economic cooperation.

CHAPTER 1

Trade Cooperation

Article 2

The two Contracting Parties confirm their determination:

(a) to take all appropriate measures to create favourable conditions for trade between them;
(b) to do their utmost to improve the structure of their trade in order to diversify it further;
(c) to examine, each for its own part and in a spirit of goodwill, any suggestions made by the other Party, in particular in the Joint Committee, for the purpose of facilitating trade between them.

Article 3

1. In their trade relations, the two Contracting Parties shall accord each other most-favoured-nation treatment in all matters regarding:

   (a) customs duties and charges of all kinds applied to the import, export, re-export, or transit of products, including the procedures for the collection of such duties or charges;
   (b) regulations, procedures and formalities concerning customs clearance, transit, warehousing and transhipment of products imported or exported;
   (c) taxes and other internal charges levied directly or indirectly on products or services imported or exported;
   (d) administrative formalities for the issue of import or export licences.

2. Paragraph 1 shall not apply in the case of:

   (a) advantages accorded by either Contracting Party to States which together with it are members of a customs union or free trade area;
   (b) advantages accorded by either Contracting Party to neighbouring countries for the purpose of facilitating border trade;
   (c) measures which either Contracting Party may take in order to meet its obligations under international commodity agreements.

Article 4

The two Contracting Parties will make every effort to foster the harmonious expansion of their reciprocal trade and to help, each by its own means, to attain a balance in such trade. Should an obvious imbalance arise, the matter must be examined within the Joint Committee so that measures can be recommended in order to improve the situation.

Article 5

1. The People's Republic of China will give favourable consideration to imports from the European Economic Community. To this end, the competent Chinese authorities will ensure that Community exporters have the possibility of participating fully in opportunities for trade with China.
2. The European Economic Community will strive for an increasing liberalization of imports from the People's Republic of China. To this end it will endeavour progressively to introduce measures extending the list of products for which imports from China have been liberalized and to increase the amounts of quotas. The procedure for implementation will be examined within the framework of the Joint Committee.

Article 6

1. The two Contracting Parties shall exchange information on any problems that may arise with regard to their trade and shall open friendly consultations, with the intention of promoting trade, for the purpose of seeking mutually satisfactory solutions to those problems. Each of the two Contracting Parties will ensure that no action is taken before consultations are held.
2. In an exceptional case, however, where the situation does not admit any delay, either Contracting Party may take measures, but must endeavour as far as possible to hold friendly consultations before doing so.
3. Each Contracting Party will ensure that when it takes the measures referred to in paragraph 2, the general objectives of this Agreement are not prejudiced.

Article 7

The two Contracting Parties undertake to promote visits by persons, groups and delegations from economic, trade and industrial circles, to facilitate industrial and technical exchanges and contracts connected with trade and to foster the organization of fairs and exhibitions by both sides and the relevant provision of services. As far as possible, they must grant each other the necessary facilities for the above activities.

Article 8

Trade in goods and the provision of services between the two Contracting Parties shall be effected at market-related prices and rates.

Article 9

The two Contracting Parties agree that payments for transactions shall be made, in accordance with their respective existing laws and regulations, in currencies of the Member States of the Community, Renminbi or any convertible currency accepted by the two parties concerned in the transactions.

CHAPTER II

Economic Cooperation

Article 10

Within the limits of their respective competence, and with the main aims of encouraging the development of industry and agriculture in the European Economic Community and in the People's Republic of China, of diversifying their economic links, encouraging scientific and technological progress, opening up new sources of supply and new markets, helping to develop their economies and raise their respective standards of living, the two Contracting Parties agree to develop economic cooperation in all the spheres subject to common accord, and in particular:

— industry and mining;
— agriculture, including agro-industry;
— science and technology;
— energy;
— transport and communication;
— environmental protection;
— cooperation in third countries.

Article 11

According to their needs and within the means at their disposal and as far as they are able, the two Contracting Parties shall encourage the application of the various forms of industrial and technical cooperation, for the benefit of their undertakings or organizations. In order to attain the objectives of this Agreement, the two Contracting Parties shall endeavour to facilitate and promote, among other activities:

— joint production and joint ventures;
— common exploitation;
— the transfer of technology;
— cooperation between financial institutions;
— visits, contact and activities designed to promote cooperation between individuals, delegations and economic organizations;
— the organization of seminars and symposia;
— consultancy services;
— technical assistance, including the training of staff;
— a continuous exchange of information relevant to commercial and economic cooperation.

Article 12

1. In order to attain the objectives of this Agreement, the two Contracting Parties shall agree, within the framework of their respective laws, rules and policies, to promote and encourage greater and mutually beneficial investment.
2. In addition, the Parties undertake to improve the existing favourable investment climate in particular through encouraging the extension, by and to the Member States of the Community and by and to the People's Republic of China, of investment promotion and protection arrangements based on the principles of equity and reciprocity.

Article 13

In view of the difference in the two Contracting Parties' levels of development, the European Economic Community is prepared, within the context of its development aid activities, within the means at its disposal, and in accordance with its rules, to continue its development activities in the

People's Republic of China. It confirms its willingness to examine the possibility of stepping up and diversifying these activities.

Article 14

Without prejudice to the relevant provisions of the Treaties establishing the European Communities, this Agreement and any action taken thereunder shall in no way affect the powers of any of the Member States of the Communities to undertake bilateral activities with the People's Republic of China in the field of economic cooperation and conclude, where appropriate, new economic cooperation agreements with the People's Republic of China.

CHAPTER III

Joint Committee

Article 15

1. The two Contracting Parties shall set up, under this Trade and Economic Cooperation Agreement, a Joint Committee comprising representatives of the European Economic Community on the one hand and representatives of the People's Republic of China on the other.
2. The tasks of the Joint Committee shall be as follows:

   — to monitor and examine the functioning of this Agreement and review the various cooperation schemes implemented;
   — to examine any questions that may arise in the implementation of this Agreement;
   — to examine problems that could hinder the development of trade and economic cooperation between the two Contracting Parties;
   — to examine means and new opportunities of developing trade and economic cooperation;
   — to make recommendations that may help to attain the objectives of this Agreement, in the areas of common interest.

3. The Joint Committee shall meet once a year, in Brussels and Beijing alternately. Extraordinary meetings may be convened by mutual agreement, at the request of either Contracting Party. The office of chairman of the Joint Committee shall be held by each of the two Contracting Parties in turn. Where both Parties consider it necessary, the Joint Committee may set up working parties to assist it in its work.

CHAPTER IV

Final Provisions

Article 16

As far as the European Economic Community is concerned, this Agreement shall apply to the territories in which the Treaty establishing the European Economic Community is applied and under the conditions laid down in that Treaty.

Article 17

This Agreement replaces the Trade Agreement between the European Economic Community and the People's Republic of China of 3 April 1978, which entered into force on 1 June 1978.

Article 18

This Agreement shall enter into force on the first day of the month following the date on which the Contracting Parties have notified each other of the completion of the legal procedures necessary for this purpose. It is concluded for a period of five years. The Agreement shall be tacitly renewed from year to year provided that neither Contracting Party notifies the other Party in writing of its denunciation of the Agreement six months before the date of expiry. However, the Agreement may be amended by mutual consent of the two Contracting Parties in order to take account of new situations.

Available from: http://ec.europa.eu/enterprise/policies/international/files/fl748_en.pdf (last accessed October 10, 2011).

APPENDIX 2

CHINA'S EU POLICY PAPER OCTOBER 2003

Foreword

The international situation has been undergoing profound changes since the advent of the new century. The trend towards world multipolarity and economic globalisation is developing amid twists and turns. Peace and development remain the themes of our era. The world is hardly a tranquil place and mankind is still confronted with many serious challenges. However, preserving world peace, promoting development and strengthening cooperation, which is vital to the well-being of all nations, represents the common aspiration of all peoples and is an irreversible trend of history.

China is committed to turning herself into a well-off society in an all-round way and aspires for a favourable international climate. China will continue to pursue its independent foreign policy of peace and work closely with other countries for the establishment of a new international political and economic order that is fair and equitable, and based on the Five Principles of Peaceful Co-existence. China will, as always, respect diversity in the world and promote democracy in international relations in the interest of world peace and common development.

The European Union (EU) is a major force in the world. The Chinese Government appreciates the importance the EU and its members attach to developing relations with China. The present EU Policy Paper of the Chinese Government is the first of its kind and aims to highlight the objectives of China's EU policy, and outline the areas and plans of cooperation and related measures in the next five years so as to enhance China-EU all-round cooperation and promote a long-term and stable development of China-EU relations.

157

Part One: Status and Role of the European Union

The creation and development of the European Union is an event of far-reaching significance following World War II. Since the launch of the European Coal and Steel Community in 1952, the EU has become what it is today through the stages of the Tax and Customs Union, the Single Market and the Economic and Monetary Union. Its integration in the foreign policy, defence and social fields has made headway. The euro has been put to circulation successfully and a single area of justice is taking shape. The EU is now a strong and the most integrated community in the world, taking up 25 and 35% of the world's economy and trade respectively and ranking high on the world's list of per capita income and foreign investment.

In 2004, the EU will be enlarged to a total membership of 25. The new European Union would then cover much of Eastern and Western Europe with an area of four million square kilometres, a population of 450 million and a GDP of over 10 trillion US Dollars.

Despite its difficulties and challenges ahead, the European integration process is irreversible and the EU will play an increasingly important role in both regional and international affairs.

Part Two: China's EU Policy

China attaches importance to the role and influence of the EU in regional and international affairs. History proves that the establishment of diplomatic relations between China and the European Economic Community in 1975 has served the interests of both sides. Despite their twists and turns, China-EU relations as a whole have been growing stronger and more mature and are now on the track of a comprehensive and sound development. In 1998 China and the EU launched their annual summit mechanism. In 2001, the two sides established a full partnership. China and the EU have developed an ever closer consultation and fruitful cooperation in the political, economic, trade, scientific, cultural and educational fields. China-EU relations now are better than any time in history.

There is no fundamental conflict of interest between China and the EU and neither side poses a threat to the other. However, given their differences in historical background, cultural heritage, political system and economic development level, it is natural that the two sides have different views or even disagree on some issues. Nevertheless China-EU relations of mutual trust and mutual benefit cannot and will not be affected if the two sides address their disagreements in a spirit of equality and mutual respect.

The common ground between China and the EU far outweighs their disagreements. Both China and the EU stand for democracy in international relations and an enhanced role of the UN. Both are committed to combating international terrorism and promoting sustainable development through poverty elimination and environmental protection endeavours. China and the EU are highly complementary economically thanks to their respective advantages. The EU has a developed economy, advanced technologies and strong financial resources while China boasts steady economic growth, a huge market and abundant labor force. There is a broad prospect for bilateral trade and economic and technological cooperation. Both China and the EU member states have a long history and splendid culture each and stand for more cultural exchanges and mutual emulation. The political, economic and cultural common understanding and interaction between China and the EU offer a solid foundation for the continued growth of China-EU relations.

To strengthen and enhance China-EU relations is an important component of China's foreign policy. China is committed to a long-term, stable and full partnership with the EU. China's EU policy objectives are:

— To promote a sound and steady development of China-EU political relations under the principles of mutual respect, mutual trust and seeking common ground while reserving differences, and contribute to world peace and stability;
— To deepen China-EU economic cooperation and trade under the principles of mutual benefit, reciprocity and consultation on an equal basis, and promote common development;
— To expand China-EU cultural and people-to-people exchanges under the principle of mutual emulation, common prosperity and complementarity, and promote cultural harmony and progress between the East and the West.

Part Three: Strengthen China-EU Cooperation in All Fields

I. *The Political Aspect*

1. Strengthen the exchange of high-level visits and political dialogue

— Maintain close contacts and timely communication between the two sides at high levels through various means.
— Give full play to the functions of the China-EU annual summit by substantiating its content, stressing its practical results and strengthening bilateral coordination.

— Implement in real earnest China-EU agreement on political dialogue and constantly improve and strengthen mechanisms of regular and irregular consultations at all levels.
— Deepen relations with all EU members, including its new ones so as to maintain stability and continuity in the overall relationship between China and EU.

2. Strictly abide by the one-China principle

The one-China principle is an important political cornerstone underpinning China-EU relations. The proper handling of the Taiwan question is essential for a steady growth of China-EU relations. China appreciates EU and its members' commitment to the one-China principle and hopes that the EU will continue to respect China's major concerns over the Taiwan question, guard against Taiwan authorities' attempt to create "two Chinas" or "one China, one Taiwan" and prudently handle Taiwan-related issues. In this connection, it is important that the EU

— Prohibit any visit by any Taiwan political figures to the EU or its member countries under whatever name or pretext; not to engage in any contact or exchange of an official or governmental nature with Taiwan authorities.
— [Does not] support Taiwan's accession to or participation in any international organization whose membership requires statehood. Taiwan's entry into the WTO in the name of "separate customs territory of Taiwan, Penghu, Jinmen, Mazu" (or Chinese Taipei for short) does not mean any change in Taiwan's status as part of China. EU exchanges with Taiwan must be strictly unofficial and non-governmental.
— [Does not] sell to Taiwan any weapon, equipment, goods, materials or technology that can be used for military purposes.

3. Encourage Hong Kong and Macao's cooperation with EU

The Central Government of China supports and encourages the Hong Kong and Macao Special Administrative Regions in developing friendly relations and cooperation with the EU in accordance with the principle of "one country, two systems" and the provisions of the two Basic Laws and on the basis of equality and mutual benefit.

4. Promote the EU's understanding of Tibet

China encourages personages of various circles in the EU to visit Tibet and welcomes the support of the EU and its members to Tibet's economic, cultural, educational and social development and their cooperation with the autonomous region subject to full respect of China's laws and regulations. The Chinese side requests the EU side not to have any contact with the "Tibetan government in exile" or provide facilities to the separatist activities of the Dalai clique.

5. Continue the human rights dialogue

There are both consensus and disagreements between China and the EU on the question of human rights. The Chinese side appreciates the EU's persistent position for dialogue and against confrontation and stands ready to continue dialogue, exchange and cooperation on human rights with the EU on the basis of equality and mutual respect so as to share information, enhance mutual understanding and deepen cooperation in protecting, *inter alia*, citizens' social and cultural rights and the rights of the disadvantaged.

6. Strengthen international cooperation

— Enhance China-EU consultation and coordination on major international and regional hotspot issues.
— Strengthen China-EU cooperation at the UN and work together to uphold the UN's authority, promote its leading role in safeguarding world peace and facilitating economic and social development, particularly in helping developing countries eliminate poverty, improving global environment and drug control, and support UN's reform.
— Advance the process of Asia-Europe cooperation. China and the EU should work together to make ASEM a role model for inter-continental cooperation on the basis of equality, a channel for exchange between the oriental and occidental civilizations and a driving force behind the establishment of a new international political and economic order.
— Jointly combat terrorism. Both China and the EU are victims of terrorism and are strongly opposed to all forms of terrorism. Both sides are also opposed to any linkage between terrorism and any particular country, nation, ethnic group or religion. China and the EU should keep in close touch and cooperation on counter-terrorism.

— Jointly safeguard the international arms control, disarmament and non-proliferation regimes and step up consultation and coordination on the basis of mutual respect; strengthen exchange and cooperation on non-proliferation and export control and the prevention of weaponization of and arms race in outer space; jointly contribute to the resolution of the issue of anti-personnel landmines and explosive remnants of war; and enhance cooperation in implementing the international arms control treaties.

7. Enhance mutual understanding between Chinese and European legislative organs

The relations between the National People's Congress of China and the parliaments of EU member countries and the European Parliament are an important link in China-EU ties. The Chinese Government welcomes and supports the enhancement of exchange and dialogue between Chinese and European legislatures on the basis of mutual respect, deeper understanding, seeking common ground while shelving differences and developing cooperation.

8. Increase exchanges between political parties in China and the EU

The Chinese Government wishes to see an increase of exchange and cooperation between the Communist Party of China and all major EU political parties, parliamentary party groups and regional organizations of political parties on the basis of independence, complete equality, mutual respect and non-interference in each other's internal affairs.

II. *The Economic Aspect*

1. Economic cooperation and trade

China is committed to developing dynamic, long-term and stable economic cooperation and trade with the EU and expects the latter to become China's largest trading and investment partner.

To this end, it is important to:

— Give play to the mechanism of the economic and trade joint committee and step up economic and trade regulatory policy dialogue; give attention to updating the Trade and Economic Cooperation

Agreement Between China and the European Union at an appropriate time; properly address irrational restrictions and technical barriers, ease restrictions on high-tech exports and tap the enormous potential of technological cooperation and trade in line with the WTO rules; grant China a full market economy status at an early date, reduce and abolish anti-dumping and other discriminatory policies and practices against China, and apply the Transitional Product-Specific Safeguard Mechanism (TPSSM) prudently; and compensate the Chinese side for its economic and trade losses which may arise due to the EU enlargement.

— Boost China-EU coordination and cooperation in the new round of WTO negotiations and work together for the success of the negotiations.

— Strengthen dialogue on investment, promote the establishment of bilateral investment-promotion institutions, energetically encourage and guide mutual investments between enterprises of the two sides, and expand cooperation between their small- and medium-sized enterprises; develop processing trade, contractual projects and labor cooperation of various kinds and encourage transnational business operation and internationalised production.

— China welcomes more EU development aid, especially in such fields as environmental protection, poverty-alleviation, public health and hygiene and education. China also welcomes a stronger and more active role of the EU in human resources development, in particular, personnel training for China's central and western regions and build-up of China's capacity of participating in [the] multilateral trading regime.

— Step up cooperation in the area of quality supervision, inspection and quarantine, establish appropriate consultation mechanisms and, subject to the principle of ensuring safety, security, hygiene, health and environmental protection, promptly address and resolve issues which may adversely affect market access of each other's products.

— Boost the customs cooperation and conclude a China-EU Customs Agreement in due course.

2. Financial cooperation

China and the EU should launch a high-level financial dialogue mechanism, expand exchanges between their central banks on policies and deepen cooperation in preventing and managing financial crises and combating the financing of terrorism and money laundering. The Chinese side welcomes an expansion of China-related business by banks of the EU countries and hopes to see an appropriate settlement of the issue of Chinese financial institutions' access to the EU market.

The Chinese side will positively examine and consider applications of EU insurance institutions for business operation in China and improve its supervisory and regulatory regime in line with the Chinese insurance laws, regulations and statutes and China's WTO commitments.

Cooperation in securities legislation, market supervision and regulation, and investment operation will be strengthened and more EU securities institutions, fund management institutions and other institutional investors will be encouraged to enter into China's market. Chinese securities institutions will be encouraged to enter into the EU's securities market when conditions are ripe. In the meantime, Chinese enterprises will be strongly supported to raise funds in the EU's securities market.

3. Agricultural cooperation

Exchanges between China and the EU in such fields as agricultural production, processing technology of agricultural produce and sustainable development will be intensified. The mechanism of the agricultural working group should be given a role to play. Bilateral cooperation between agricultural research institutes, universities and colleges as well as enterprises should be pushed forward. EU Enterprises are encouraged to take an active part in agricultural development in China's central and western regions and invest in such fields as agricultural high and new technologies, intensive processing of agricultural produce and development of agricultural infrastructure.

4. Environmental cooperation

China-EU communication and cooperation in environmental protection should be stimulated and a mechanism of dialogue between the Chinese and EU environmental ministers launched. Framework documents on environmental cooperation should be formulated, and discussions held on the establishment of information network on environmental cooperation. Bilateral cooperation should be strengthened on such issues as environmental legislation and management, climate change, bio-diversity protection, bio-safety management, and trade and environment. Efforts should be made to jointly promote the implementation of the follow-up actions of the World Summit on Sustainable Development in Johannesburg. Non-governmental environmental protection organizations are encouraged to develop mutual exchanges. EU enterprises are encouraged to gain more access to [the] Chinese environmental protection market through fair competition.

5. IT cooperation

The Chinese side would like to see EU participation in China's IT promotion. The mechanism of the EU-China working group on information society will be strengthened. Exchanges and dialogue will be conducted on strategies, policies, rules and regulations of information society. Trade in IT products and industrial and technological cooperation will be actively boosted. Greater exchanges in intellectual property rights and technical standards will be encouraged. Cooperation in the field of "Digital Olympics" will be promoted.

6. Energy cooperation

China-EU cooperation will be expanded in such fields as energy structure, clean energy, renewable energy, and energy efficiency and saving. Exchanges on energy development policies will be promoted. Efforts will be made to ensure a successful EU-China Energy Conference. The energy working group mechanism will be strengthened. Training on energy technology and cooperation in demonstration projects will be boosted to promote application and transfer of technology.

7. Transport cooperation

A mechanism of China-EU regular meeting will be set up within the framework of the China-EU Agreement on Maritime Transport. Cooperation in maritime transport and other maritime fields will be developed and coordination and cooperation in international organizations such as the International Maritime Organization (IMO) will be strengthened. Bilateral exchanges will be deepened and broadened in respect of policies of inland river transport, navigation safety and shipping standardization. Cooperation and exchanges in highway technology and management will be expanded. Dialogue and exchanges on highway transport legislation will be strengthened.

China-EU exchanges in civil aviation will be deepened. Chinese and EU enterprises are encouraged to strengthen their cooperation on production, technology, management and training.

III. *The Education, Science-Technology, Culture, Health and Other Aspects*

1. Cooperation in science and technology

It is essential to promote China-EU scientific and technological cooperation on the basis of the principles of mutual benefit and reciprocity, sharing of results and protection of intellectual property rights. Joint development and cooperation on generic technologies and major technical equipment should be stepped up and Chinese institutions are encouraged to participate in the EU Framework Programme for Research and Technological Development. China will, on the premise of equality and mutual benefit and a balance between interests and obligations, participate in the Galileo Programme and enhance cooperation in international "big science" projects. Full play should be given to the role of the Scientific and Technologic Cooperation Steering Committee and efforts should be made to ensure a successful China-Europe Science & Technology and Innovation Policy Forum. Cooperation between scientific and technological intermediary agencies of the two sides as well as the interflow and training of scientific and technological human resources should be encouraged. Support should be given to Chinese and EU enterprises in their involvement in scientific and technological cooperation.

2. Cultural exchange

China will be more open in cementing and deepening its exchange and cooperation with EU members in the cultural field and work towards a multi-level and all-dimensional framework of cultural exchanges between China and the European Union, EU members and their respective local governments, and between their peoples and business communities so as to make it easier for the people of China and the EU to get to know each other's fine cultures.

China will establish Chinese cultural centres in capitals of EU members and the EU headquarters — Brussels. On the basis of reciprocity and mutual benefit, China welcomes the set-up of cultural centres in Beijing by the EU side. China will encourage high quality cultural exchange activities and explore new modalities of cooperation in culture-related industries. Discussions will be held on the formation of a China-EU cultural cooperation consultation mechanism and the idea of jointly holding a China-EU cultural forum.

3. Cooperation in education

Exchanges at all levels will be enhanced and expanded. It is necessary to establish a China-EU education cooperation consultation mechanism as appropriate and strengthen cooperation in areas including mutual recognition of academic credentials and degrees, exchange of students, language teaching, exchange of scholarships and teacher training. Work should be done to make a success of the China-Europe International Business School and bring forth more top professionals. The teaching of each other's languages should be encouraged and supported.

4. Cooperation in health and medical care

Cooperation in the health sector should be strengthened, particularly in sharing experience of prevention and control of SARS, HIV/AIDS and other serious diseases. Efforts should be made to develop exchanges in clinical diagnosis and treatment, epidemiological investigation, analysis and surveillance, laboratory testing, R&D for medicines and vaccines, and training of medical personnel. Exploratory endeavour should be made for the establishment of a mechanism to keep each other informed and provide technical support in case of emergent public health hazards.

5. Press exchange

Exchanges and cooperation will be boosted between the press and media communities of the two sides. Chinese and EU media agencies should be encouraged to enhance mutual understanding and give comprehensive and unbiased reports of each other. Relevant government departments or agencies of the two sides should enhance mutual contact and communication and share practices and experience in respect of government press release and the handling of government-media relations.

6. Personnel exchange

People-to-people exchanges and those between non-governmental organi-zations of China and the EU should be encouraged. China is ready to conclude as early as possible agreement on designating EU countries as tourism destinations for outbound Chinese citizens in compliance with the principles of equality, reciprocity and mutual benefit.

China-EU consular cooperation should be strengthened and expanded. An early solution should be found through consultations to the problem of difficult access to entry visas by Chinese citizens and their impeded entry into EU countries. The legitimate rights and interests of travellers should be protected. Normal people-to-people exchanges between China and the EU should be ensured.

It is imperative to combat illegal migration and human trafficking, strictly enforce laws and crack down on illegal activities and crimes. The two sides should increase consultations and coordination and appropri-ately handle the question of repatriation and other issues arising there from.

IV. *The Social, Judicial and Administrative Aspects*

1. Cooperation in labor and social security

China and the EU should strengthen cooperation on employment of legal immigrants and protection of the rights and interests of migrant workers and enhance coordination in international labor affairs. The two sides will negotiate and conclude a bilateral social security agreement and imple-ment their joint social security cooperation programme as well as broaden exchanges in social insurance of various kinds.

2. Exchange in judicial field

It is necessary to continue with the China-EU cooperation programme in the legal and judicial fields based on equality and mutual respect, broaden related areas of cooperation, enhance exchanges in judicial reform and other key areas and explore cooperation with respect to administration of justice in combating cross border crimes. The two sides should do more in sharing experience of legal supervision and explore the possibility of estab-lishing a mechanism of annual meeting between their high-level judicial officials.

3. Cooperation in police affairs

The Chinese side will establish and strengthen exchanges with relevant EU agencies and EUROPOL, broaden substantial cooperation with law-enforcement organs of EU members and step up coordination in case handling and information sharing within their respective legal framework. The two sides should support and actively participate in UN peacekeeping and other activities.

4. Cooperation in public administration

China and the EU should share experience in transforming government functions and deepening personnel management reform, discuss the establishment of a China-EU cooperation mechanism on personnel and administrative management and conduct exchanges in civil service system building and human resources development.

V. *The Military Aspect*

China and the EU will maintain high-level military-to-military exchanges, develop and improve, step by step, a strategic security consultation mechanism, exchange more missions of military experts, and expand exchanges in respect of military officers' training and defence studies.

The EU should lift its ban on arms sales to China at an early date so as to remove barriers to greater bilateral cooperation on defence industry and technologies.

Available from: http://www.fmprc.gov.cn/eng/topics/ceupp/t27708.htm (last accessed October 10, 2011).

APPENDIX 3

COMMUNICATION FROM THE COMMISSION TO THE COUNCIL AND THE EUROPEAN PARLIAMENT

EU-CHINA: CLOSER PARTNERS, GROWING RESPONSIBILITIES

1. What is at stake?

China has re-emerged as a major power in the last decade. It has become the world's fourth economy and third exporter, but also an increasingly important political power. China's economic growth has thrown weight behind a significantly more active and sophisticated Chinese foreign policy. China's desire to grow and seek a place in the world commensurate with its political and economic power is a central tenet of its policy. Given China's size and phenomenal growth, these changes have a profound impact on global politics and trade.

The EU offers the largest market in the world. It is home to a global reserve currency. It enjoys world leadership in key technologies and skills. The EU plays a central role in finding sustainable solutions to today's challenges, on the environment, on energy, on globalisation. It has proved capable of exerting a progressive influence well beyond its borders and is the world's largest provider of development aid.

Europe needs to respond effectively to China's renewed strength. To tackle the key challenges facing Europe today — including climate change, employment, migration, security — we need to leverage the potential of a dynamic relationship with China based on our values. We also have an interest in supporting China's reform process. This means factoring the China dimension into the full range of EU policies, external and internal. It also means close co-ordination inside the EU to ensure an overall and coherent approach.

171

To better reflect the importance of their relations, the EU and China agreed a strategic partnership in 2003. Some differences remain, but are being managed effectively, and relations are increasingly mature and realistic. At the same time China is, with the EU, closely bound to the globalisation process and becoming more integrated into the international system.

The EU's fundamental approach to China must remain one of engagement and partnership. But with a closer strategic partnership, mutual responsibilities increase. The partnership should meet both sides' interests and the EU and China need to work together as they assume more active and responsible international roles, supporting and contributing to a strong and effective multilateral system. The goal should be a situation where China and the EU can bring their respective strengths to bear to offer joint solutions to global problems.

Both the EU and China stand to gain from our trade and economic partnership. If we are to recognise its full potential, closing Europe's doors to Chinese competition is not the answer. But to build and maintain political support for openness towards China, the benefits of engagement must be fully realised in Europe. China should open its own markets and ensure conditions of fair market competition. Adjusting to the competitive challenge and driving a fair bargain with China will be the central challenge of EU trade policy in the decade to come. This key bilateral challenge provides a litmus test for our partnership, and is set out in more detail in a trade policy paper entitled "Competition and Partnership" which accompanies the present Communication.

Europe and China can do more to promote their own interests together than they will ever achieve apart.

2. Context: China's Revival

Internal stability remains the key driver for Chinese policy. Over recent decades, stability has been underpinned by delivery of strong economic growth. Since 1980 China has enjoyed 9% annual average growth and has seen its share of world GDP expand tenfold to reach 5% of global GDP. China's growth has resulted in the steepest recorded drop in poverty in world history, and the emergence of a large middle class, better educated and with rising purchasing power and choices.

But the story of this phenomenal growth masks uncertainties and fragility. The Chinese leadership treads a complex daily path, facing a range of important challenges, primarily domestic, but which increasingly resonate beyond national boundaries:

- Disparities continue to grow. The wealth gap is significant and growing, as are social, regional and gender imbalances; there is huge stress on healthcare and education systems; and China is already facing significant demographic shifts and the challenges of a rapidly ageing population;
- China's demand for energy and raw materials — China is already the world's second largest energy consumer — is already significant and will continue to grow; and the environmental cost of untrammelled economic and industrial growth is becoming more and more apparent. At the same time growth patterns have not been balanced, with a focus on exports to the detriment of domestic demand.

Growth remains central to China's reform agenda, but increasingly is tempered with measures to address social inequality and ensure more sustainable economic and political development. Paradoxically, in a number of areas, the conditions for stability improve as the Party and State relax control. A more independent judiciary, a stronger civil society, a freer press will ultimately encourage stability, providing necessary checks and balances. Recognition of the need for more balanced development, building a "harmonious society", is encouraging. But further reform will be necessary.

China's regional and international policy also supports domestic imperatives: a secure and peaceful neighbourhood is one conducive to economic growth; and China's wider international engagement remains characterised by pursuit of very specific objectives, including securing the natural resources needed to power growth. At the same time we have seen China's desire to build international respect and recognition. The 2008 Olympic Games in Beijing and the 2010 World Expo in Shanghai will focus the world's attention on China's progress.

China has traditionally described its foreign policy as one of strict non-interference, but as it takes on a more active and assertive international role, this becomes increasingly untenable. The Chinese government is beginning to recognise this, and the international responsibilities commensurate to its economic importance and role as a permanent member of the UN Security Council as illustrated by its increasingly active diplomatic commitments.

The EU and China benefit from globalisation and share common interests in its success. It presents challenges to both and brings further responsibilities. We also share a desire to see an effective multilateral system. But there remain divergences in values, on which dialogue must continue.

As the partnership strengthens, expectations and responsibilities on both sides increase. As China's biggest trading partner, EU trade policy has an important impact on China, as do China's policies on the EU. Increasingly, both sides expect that impact to be taken into account in their partner's policy formulation.

3. The Way Forward

The EU should continue support for China's internal political and economic reform process, for a strong and stable China which fully respects fundamental rights and freedoms, protects minorities and guarantees the rule of law. The EU will reinforce cooperation to ensure sustainable development, pursue a fair and robust trade policy and work to strengthen and add balance to bilateral relations. The EU and China should work together in support of peace and stability. The EU should increase co-ordination and joint action and improve cooperation with European industry and civil society.

Until now the legal basis for relations has been the 1985 Trade and Cooperation Agreement. This no longer reflects the breadth and scope of the relationship and at the 9th EU-China Summit leaders agreed to launch negotiations on a new, extended Partnership and Cooperation Agreement (PCA) to update the basis for our cooperation. This new agreement presents an important opportunity. It will provide a single framework covering the full range and complexity of our relationship, and at the same time should be forward-looking and reflect the priorities outlined in this Communication.

3.1. *Supporting China's Transition Towards a More Open and Plural Society*

The Chinese leadership has repeatedly stated its support for reform, including on basic rights and freedoms. But in this area progress on the ground has been limited. The EU must consider how it can most effectively assist China's reform process, making the case that better protection of human rights, a more open society, and more accountable government would be beneficial to China, and essential for continued economic growth.

Democracy, human rights and the promotion of common values remain fundamental tenets of EU policy and of central importance to bilateral relations. The EU should support and encourage the development of a full, healthy and independent civil society in China. It should support efforts to strengthen the rule of law — an essential basis for all other reform.

At the same time, the EU will continue to encourage full respect of fundamental rights and freedoms in all regions of China; freedom of speech, religion and association, the right to a fair trial and the protection of minorities call for particular attention — in all regions of China. The EU will also encourage China to be an active and constructive partner in the Human Rights Council, holding China to the values which the UN embraces, including the International Covenant on Civil and Political Rights.

The twice-yearly human rights dialogue was conceived at an earlier stage in EU-China relations. It remains fit for purpose, but the EU's expectations — which have increased in line with the quality of our partnership — are increasingly not being met. The dialogue should be:

- more focused and results-oriented, with higher quality exchanges and concrete results;
- more flexible, taking on input from separate seminars and sub-groups;
- better co-ordinated with Member State dialogues.

3.2. *Sustainable Development*

One of today's key global challenges is to ensure our development is sustainable. China will be central to meeting this challenge. China's domestic reform policy is important and the Commission will continue to support this through its cooperation programme, including corporate social responsibility. On issues such as energy, the environment and climate change, respect for international social standards, development assistance, as well as wider macroeconomic issues, the EU and China should ensure close international cooperation. Both sides should:

Ensure secure and sustainable energy supplies. As important players in world energy markets, the EU and China share a common interest and responsibility in ensuring the security and sustainability of energy supplies, improving efficiency and mitigating the environmental impact of energy production and consumption. The EU's priority should be to ensure China's integration into world energy markets and multilateral governance mechanisms and institutions, and to encourage China to become an active and responsible energy partner. On that basis both sides should work together to:

- increase international cooperation, in particular efforts to improve transparency and reliability of energy data and the exchange of information aimed at improving energy security in developing countries, including Africa;
- strengthen China's technical and regulatory expertise, reducing growth in energy demand, increasing energy efficiency and use of clean renewable energy such as wind, biomass and bio fuels, promoting energy standards and savings through the development and deployment of near zero emission coal technology;
- commit to enhance stability through a market-based approach to investment and procurement; dialogue with other major consumers; encouragement of transparent and non-discriminatory regulatory frameworks, including open and effective energy market access; and by promoting the adoption of internationally recognised norms and standards.

Combat climate change and improve the environment. We already have a good basis for cooperation on environment issues and on climate change through the Partnership established at the 2005 EU-China Summit.

- The EU should share regulatory expertise, working with China to prevent pollution, safeguard biodiversity, make the use of energy, water and raw materials more efficient, and improve transparency and the enforcement of environmental legislation. Both sides should work together to tackle deforestation and illegal logging, sustainable management of fisheries resources and maritime governance;
- Both sides should build on the Climate Change Partnership, reinforcing bilateral cooperation, and strengthening international cooperation, meeting shared international responsibilities under the Climate Change Convention and Kyoto Protocol and engage actively in the dialogues on international climate change cooperation post-2012. We should strengthen the use of emissions trading and clean development mechanisms.

Improve exchanges on employment and social issues. China is committed to tackle social disparities and promote more balanced development. The EU and China should:

- intensify cooperation on employment and social issues reinforcing and expanding bilateral dialogue to include issues such as health and safety at work, decent work standards, and meeting the challenges of an ageing population;
- work together to ensure that international commitments on labor and social issues are upheld.

Improve co-ordination on international development. Closer cooperation on international development issues would benefit the EU, China and partners in the developing world. There are significant downsides if we are not able to co-ordinate effectively, particularly in Africa but also in other developing countries. The EU and China should:

- engage in a structured dialogue on Africa's sustainable development. There should be transparency on the activity and priorities of both sides, providing a basis for full discussion;
- support regional efforts to improve governance in Africa;
- explore opportunities for improving China's integration into international efforts to improve aid efficiency, co-ordination and opportunities for practical bilateral cooperation on the ground.

Build sustainable economic growth. China has become a source [of] growth for the EU and the world, but China's current growth model is also the source of important imbalances in EU-China trade. The Chinese government has recognised the importance of meeting macroeconomic challenges, of forward-looking fiscal, monetary and structural policies, boosting consumption and reducing inequalities. Increasing exchange rate flexibility will be an important factor, helping rebalance growth towards domestic demand and increasing Chinese households' purchasing power. Policies which would lead to a reduction of its current account surplus would increase China's control of its economy and contain risks of overheating, and at the same time meet China's shared responsibility to ensure a stable and balanced world economy.

As key economic powers, the EU and China should further develop their partnership and work together to tackle global economic issues; they should:

- deepen cooperation and share experience in formulating and implementing monetary, fiscal, financial, exchange rate and structural policies;

- co-operate towards the orderly unwinding of global imbalances;
- strengthen and upgrade their macroeconomic dialogue.

3.3. *Trade and Economic Relations*

China's integration into the global trading system has benefited both Europe and China. The EU is China's largest trading partner, representing more than 19% of China's external trade. European companies trading with and investing in China have contributed to China's growth, bringing capital goods, knowledge and technology that have been instrumental to China's development.

An economically strong China is in Europe's interest. China, especially its rapidly increasing middle class, is a growing market for EU exports. EU exports to China increased by over 100% between 2000 and 2005, much faster than its exports to the rest of the world. EU exports of services to China expanded six-fold in the ten years to 2004. European companies and consumers benefit from competitively priced Chinese inputs and consumer goods. Openness brings benefits to both China and the EU.

Nevertheless, in Europe there is a growing perception that China's as yet incomplete implementation of WTO obligations and new barriers to market access are preventing a genuinely reciprocal trading relationship. Imports from China have added to pressure to adjust to globalisation in Europe. This trend is likely to continue as China moves up the value chain.

For the relationship to be politically and economically sustainable in the long term, Europe should continue to offer open and fair access to China's exports and to adjust to the competitive challenge. The EU needs to develop and consolidate areas of comparative advantage in high-value and high-tech design and production and to help workers retrain. China for its part should reciprocate by strengthening its commitment to open markets and fair competition. Both sides should address concern over the impact of economic growth on natural resources and the environment. The EU will:

Insist on openness. The EU will continue working with China towards the full implementation of its WTO obligations and will urge China to move beyond its WTO commitments in further opening its market to create opportunities for EU companies. The EU will accept that it cannot demand openness from China from behind barriers of its own. The EU will urge China to honour its commitment to open accession negotiations on the Government Procurement Agreement in 2008 and work to bring them to a successful conclusion as rapidly as possible.

Level the playing field. Better protection of intellectual property rights in China and ending forced technology transfers are EU priorities, including through implementation by China of WTO obligations and will help create a better investment climate in China. The EU will press China to stop granting prohibited subsidies and reform its banking system, and encourage China to allow market forces to operate in its trade in raw materials.

Support European companies. The Commission will make a major effort to assist companies doing business with China, in particular small and medium sized enterprises while urging them to respect decent work standards. The EU will extend and strengthen the existing information, training and advice on protecting and defending IPR in China. A European Centre in Beijing should be opened. The EU-China Managers Exchange and Training Programme should be extended.

Defend the EU's interests: dialogue first. The EU has a clear preference for resolving trade irritants with China through dialogue and negotiation. The existing EU-China trade related dialogues should be strengthened at all levels, their focus should be sharpened on facilitating trade and improving market access and their scope extended. The EU and China also have an interest in joining their efforts in international rule making and global standard setting bodies. The EU will actively pursue global supervisory and regulatory solutions, promoting open markets and regulatory convergence, and build on cooperation with China through EU-China regulatory dialogues. This will also help to ensure compliance of Chinese imports with EU standards for food and non-food products.

But where other efforts have failed, the Commission will use the WTO dispute settlement system to ensure compliance with multilaterally agreed rules and obligations. Trade defence measures will remain an instrument to ensure fair conditions of trade. The EU is actively working with China with a view to creating the conditions which would permit early granting of MES. Recent progress has been made on some of the conditions. The Commission will continue to work with the Chinese authorities through the mechanisms we have established and will be ready to act quickly once all the conditions are met.

Build a stronger relationship. A key objective of the negotiations for a new Partnership and Cooperation Agreement, which will also update the 1985 Trade and cooperation Agreement, will be better access to the Chinese market for European exporters and investors, going beyond WTO commitments, better protection of intellectual property and mutual recognition of geographical indications. China is already a major beneficiary of the international trading system and should assume a responsibility commensurate with those benefits, making a substantial contribution to reviving and completing the WTO Doha Round.

Many of these steps are not only in EU's interest. They are strongly in China's interest and an integral part of China's progress towards balanced and sustainable growth and development and global leadership and responsibility. The accompanying trade policy paper sets out a comprehensive approach to EU-China trade and investment relations for the medium term.

3.4. *Strengthening Bilateral Cooperation*

Bilateral cooperation spans a wide range of issues, including 7 formal Agreements, 22 sectoral dialogues, covering diverse and important issues from aviation and maritime transport to regional and macroeconomic policy. Further development of the structured dialogue to exchange experiences and views on competition matters, as well as technical and capacity-building assistance as regards competition enforcement, remains important. Cooperation has been successful and positive. But more must be done to focus cooperation and ensure balance and mutual benefit, in all areas, but particularly on flagship areas such as science and technology cooperation. More should be done to strengthen cooperation on migration issues, people-to-people links, and the structures governing our official relations. Both sides should:

Ensure quality and increased cooperation in science and technology. Science and technology cooperation is a priority area for the Chinese government. China spends 1.5% of its GDP on a dynamic and growing research and development programme. Bilateral cooperation is also strong: China is one of the most important third countries participating in more EU research projects under the 6th Research Framework Programme, giving it access to 600 million euros of research, and China is an important partner on key projects such as ITER and Galileo. EU participation in Chinese programmes should be increased.

The Joint Declaration from the Science and Technology Forum in May 2005 set the context for taking cooperation forward, based on mutual benefit and reciprocal access and participation. Both sides should:

- consolidate and improve the visibility of cooperation. This will allow both sides to focus and set priorities effectively and to respond to dynamic issues such as emerging pandemics or work on clean energy technologies; make it easier to examine scope for increased reciprocity; and provide a basis for more effective co-ordination with Member States;

- improve joint planning to ensure mutual benefit, and increase flexibility to fund the participation of European researchers in Chinese research programmes. Both sides should facilitate researchers' mobility which in the case of the EU is promoted through specific grants under the Framework Programme.

Build an effective migration relationship. Chinese and other migrants enrich the EU culturally and bring with them important skills and expertise. But there is a significant downside if the process is not managed effectively. There has to be an effective legal framework to facilitate people-to-people exchanges. But we need effective mechanisms to deal with those who abuse the system, with a focus on prevention and return. Both sides should work towards the early conclusion of an effective Readmission Agreement.

- The existing consultation mechanism should continue and be extended to cover both legal and illegal migration, and with renewed political commitment to make progress;
- Both sides should agree and push forward specific cooperation projects on e.g. the exchange of officials and training; and there should be exchanges on biometric technology;
- There should be a dedicated dialogue with the Ministry of Public Security covering migration and the fight against organised crime, terrorism and corruption;
- The EU-China Tourism Agreement (ADS) will need continued proactive and practical cooperation to ensure it functions effectively.

Expand people-to-people links. We should strengthen the full range of people-to-people links which underpin our relations through significant and sustained action on both sides, from cultural exchanges and tourism to civil society and academic links.

- *Civil society* and institutional links should provide direct support and impetus for political and trade relations. Both sides should facilitate direct links between civil society groups in the EU and China in all areas, and include them in sectoral dialogues where possible. Official non-governmental links should be strengthened and expanded. The

European Parliament plays a central role and should expand cooperation with the Chinese National People's Congress. The EU should also strengthen links between ECOSOC and the Chinese Economic and Social Committee, political parties, and between other semi-official bodies.

- *Education* has been an area of particular success, with 170 000 Chinese students studying in the EU in 2005. We should continue to build on existing cooperation through programmes run by individual Member States and through the China-specific strand of the Erasmus Mundus programme. There have been positive examples of work to set up joint degree courses and joint campuses. We should also implement specific projects such as a European Law School. Both sides will continue to encourage EU students to study in China. To strengthen language capability, the Commission will support a specific programme to train Chinese language teachers to teach in Europe.

- *Academic expertise* in the EU on China needs to be improved and co-ordinated more effectively. Action is needed by both sides to support effective interaction between European and Chinese academia. The Commission should continue to support an academic network on China, drawing together academic expertise to inform EU policy and co-ordinating information-sharing within the academic community; and there should be a small number of prestigious professorships on Chinese studies created and made available to European universities. There should be a permanent regular dialogue between European and Chinese think tanks.

Make bilateral structures more effective. Both sides should reflect on the structures which govern relations and consider whether they should be streamlined, improved or upgraded. The Commission's 2003 Policy Paper sought to expand sectoral dialogue between the EU and China. This has been very successful, and the majority function well and make an important contribution to our partnership. But progress should be reviewed. Both sides should also consider whether there are new bodies or mechanisms which would further contribute to EU-China relations.

- Annual Summits provide a good framework for maintaining contacts at head of government level. This should be supported by regular cross-cutting exchange and dialogue at technical, ministerial and more senior level. In addition, both sides should explore further options for flexible and informal opportunities to meet and exchange views;

- The recently agreed strategic dialogue at Vice Foreign Minister level should be a key mechanism covering regional and geo-political issues and adding focus, impact and value to the relationship;
- Both sides should undertake a thorough examination of the rationale, interrelationship and performance of the sectoral dialogues with the aim of maximising synergies and ensuring mutual benefit, and ensure interested stakeholders are involved where possible. The Commission will produce a series of Working Documents on specific sectoral challenges;
- A new independent EU-China Forum should be set up. On the EU side it should be at arms length from the institutions and should draw on civil society, academic, business and cultural expertise, providing policy input to political leaders and impetus to bilateral relations.

The EU should ensure that it speaks with one voice on the panoply of issues related to its relations with China. Given the complexity of the relationship and the importance of continuity, regular, systematic and cross-cutting internal co-ordination will be essential.

The EU's cooperation programme, delivered through the country strategy paper (CSP) and national indicative programmes, should continue to play a role in supporting the partnership between the two sides and China's reform process. But as China moves further away from the status of a typical recipient of overseas development aid, the EU must calibrate its cooperation programme carefully and keep it under review. cooperation must be in both sides' interests, reflect the EU's own principles and values, and serve to underpin the partnership.

3.5. *International and Regional Cooperation*

The EU and China have an interest in promoting peace and security through a reformed and effective multilateral system. They should co-operate closely in the framework of the UN, working to find multilateral solutions to emerging crises, and to combat terrorism and increase regional cooperation, including through involvement by both in emerging regional structures. This common interest, in strong multilateralism, peace and security should also be reflected in closer cooperation and more structured dialogue on the Middle East, Africa and East Asia, and on cross-cutting challenges such as non-proliferation.

East Asia. It is clear the EU has a significant interest in the strategic security situation in East Asia. It should build on the increasing effectiveness of its foreign and security policy and its strategic interest in the region by drawing up public guidelines for its policy.

China has a key role to play in the region and has been working to improve relations with its neighbours, including Russia and India, and with central Asia through the Shanghai Cooperation Organisation. But there remains scope for improvement in Sino-Japanese relations. The EU has an interest in strong relations between the region's major players and in continued regional integration.

Taiwan. The EU has a significant stake in the maintenance of cross-straits peace and stability. On the basis of its One China Policy, and taking account of the strategic balance in the region, the EU should continue to take an active interest, and to make its views known to both sides. Policy should take account of the EU's:

- opposition to any measure which would amount to a unilateral change of the status quo;
- strong opposition to the use of force;
- encouragement for pragmatic solutions and confidence building measures;
- support for dialogue between all parties; and,
- continuing strong economic and trade links with Taiwan.

Transparency on Chinese military expenditure and objectives. There is increasing concern caused by the opacity of China's defence expenditure. As expenditure continues to increase, China needs to be convinced of the importance of improving transparency. At the same time, the EU should improve its analytical capacity on China's military development.

Arms embargo. The arms embargo was put in place as a result of events in Tiananmen Square in 1989. The EU has agreed to continue to work towards embargo lift, but further work will be necessary by both sides:

- Current and incoming Presidencies should finalise technical preparations to ensure [a] lift would not lead to a qualitative or quantitative increase in arms sales, and continue to explore possibilities for building a consensus for lift. The EU should work with China to improve the atmosphere for lift, making progress on China's human rights situation; working to improve cross-straits relations; and by improving the transparency of its military expenditure.

Non-proliferation. Non-proliferation represents a key area for the strategic partnership. International and bilateral cooperation is based on UNSCR 1540 and the Joint Declaration on Non-Proliferation agreed at the 2004 EU-China Summit. The EU is supportive of China's central role in work on the Korean peninsula and continued Chinese support will be crucial to progress on the Iranian nuclear issue. There has been a good start on dialogue and practical cooperation to strengthen and enforce export controls. The EU should build on this, working with Chinese officials to encourage China to:

- comply with all non-proliferation and disarmament treaties and international instruments, and to promote compliance with them regionally and internationally;
- strengthen export controls of WMD-related materials, equipment and technologies as well as of conventional weapons and small arms and light weapons.

Both sides should work together to share practical experience in implementing and enforcing export controls, including through training for Chinese customs officials. They should consider scope for joint EU/Asia initiatives in the context of the ASEAN Regional Forum.

4. Conclusion

China is one the EU's most important partners. China's re-emergence is a welcome phenomenon. But to respond positively and effectively, the EU must improve policy co-ordination at all levels, and ensure a focused single European voice on key issues.

We have a strong and growing bilateral relationship. But we must continue build on this. The recommendations in this Communication, which the Council is invited to endorse and complement through Council Conclusions, represent a challenging agenda for the EU to do so, and the Partnership and Cooperation Agreement provides an important practical mechanism to move this agenda forward.

A closer, stronger strategic partnership is in the EU's and China's interests. But with this comes an increase in responsibilities, and a need for openness which will require concerted action by both sides.

Available from: http://eur-lex.europa.eu/LexUriServ/LexUriServ.do?uri=COM:2006:0631:FIN:EN:PDF (last accessed October 10, 2011).

INDEX